Social Responsibility
in Farm Leadership

This book is One of a Series on Ethics and Economic Life
Originated by a Study Committee of the Federal Council of Churches
Subsequently Merged in the National Council of Churches

Charles P. Taft, Chairman,
Department of the Church and Economic Life

Cameron P. Hall, Executive Director

TOWARD AN UNDERSTANDING OF THE ETHICS AND
ECONOMICS OF SOCIETY

Already Published

GOALS OF ECONOMIC LIFE
Edited by A. Dudley Ward

THE ORGANIZATIONAL REVOLUTION
By Kenneth E. Boulding

SOCIAL RESPONSIBILITIES OF THE BUSINESSMAN
By Howard R. Bowen

AMERICAN INCOME AND ITS USE
By Elizabeth E. Hoyt, Margaret G. Reid, Joseph L. McConnell,
and Janet M. Hooks

CHRISTIAN VALUES AND ECONOMIC LIFE
By Howard R. Bowen, John C. Bennett, William Adams Brown, Jr.,
and G. Bromley Oxnam

THE AMERICAN ECONOMY—ATTITUDES AND OPINIONS
By A. Dudley Ward

SOCIAL RESPONSIBILITY IN FARM LEADERSHIP
By Walter W. Wilcox

Other Volumes in Preparation

Social Responsibility in Farm Leadership

An Analysis of Farm Problems and Farm Leadership in Action

By Walter W. Wilcox

HARPER & BROTHERS · PUBLISHERS · NEW YORK

This volume has been prepared under the direction of a study group authorized by the Federal Council of Churches in 1949. In 1950 the Federal Council was merged into the National Council of Churches. The Federal Council has retained its corporate entity and continues to hold the copyright. The National Council of Churches points out that the volume is not a statement or pronouncement of the National Council. The author is solely responsible for its contents.

Contents

Foreword

by CHARLES P. TAFT

Chairman of the Department of the Church and Economic Life and of Its Study Committee

This volume forms part of a larger study of Christian Ethics and Economic Life which was begun in 1949 by the Department of the Church and Economic Life of the Federal Council of the Churches of Christ in America. At the beginning of 1951 the Federal Council was merged with other interdenominational agencies to form the National Council of the Churches of Christ in the United States of America, made up of thirty Protestant and Orthodox church bodies within the United States.

In recent years religious leaders have recognized that the ethical problems of economic life have become increasingly urgent. The ethics of everyday decisions and practices in economic life, private and public, where we earn our living are matters of wide public concern. We need to go behind observed individual acts and group pressures for a deeper understanding of the motives underlying what people do in their economic activities, of how the system fits together, and of how close our preconceived ideas are to reality.

Change is dominant in our national life and perhaps nowhere so much so as in its economic aspects. During the past half-century our ways of life and work have undergone a vast alteration. This change has been accomplished without violence and without great apparent upset, but the tempo of its pace is revolutionary. Certainly if people whose span of life was in the nineteenth century could see what we see in everyday life, they would hardly accept any word but revolution for the process that has brought it about.

This accelerated change demands for all thoughtful people an understanding of the effects of this revolution upon ethics and human values. How shall we deal with the dynamism in our economic life so as to preserve and extend the dignity of the individual, respect for the rights of minorities, sensitivity to the public welfare, and free discussion and peaceful persuasion? We cannot rely upon

vii

business statistics to measure these intangibles. Judgments of even the best qualified individuals about actual or impending changes, affected as opinions are by individual temperament, vested interests, or political partisanship, are also inadequate if considered separately. The fullest use of all our resources for information and discussion is required for sound progress toward solution of our complex problems.

There is no vital threat to our inherited and cherished values either in the *status quo* or in change as such. We cannot take ethics into the stratosphere and separate it from practical economic concerns. What is needed is a better understanding both of economic facts and also of those ethical convictions and values which have special significance in the meaning and direction they should give to economic activity.

In many parts of the world we find a fanatic cynicism or a false philosophy in opposition to the foundations upon which Western society is based. What earlier generations took for granted, such as the value and integrity of the individual, the character of government as a tool for service of the people, the capacity of human life for essential decency and justice—these are now challenged with emotional zeal in the name of conflicting assumptions claimed also to be moral or at least essential for an efficient society.

Here lies the real crisis of the second half of the present century. We must meet this challenge, in so far as it is evil, and clarify in relation to our own institutions the basic ethical affirmations which we support.

The Federal Council of Churches conducted for many years an educational program on the ethical issues involved in economic life. Many denominational bodies have likewise been active in this field. It has become clear, however, that we need a more careful and realistic investigation of economic life and its relation to spiritual and moral values in a Christian frame of reference. We need to make use of the capacities of social scientists and theologians, in close association with other persons drawn from many occupations.

Accordingly, as a beginning of such an investigation, a three-year study was commenced in 1949 under a grant from the Rockefeller Foundation, and the study was continued under a further grant from the same source in 1952. The Foundation has not sought to exercise any supervisory control over the study and does not assume responsibility for any of the findings. The results of the study so far are presented in seven volumes: *Goals of Economic Life, The Organizational Revolution, Social Responsibilities of the Businessman, American Income and Its Use, The American Economy—Attitudes and Opinions, Christian Values and Economic Life,* and *Social Responsibility in Farm Leadership.* Among the other volumes planned are three which continue the social responsibilities theme with respect to labor organizations, mass communicators, and the churches themselves and their agencies in so far as economic policies and practices are concerned. Another volume is being prepared by a group of faculty members at Wesleyan University on public policy formation in a democratic society in relation to economic growth. The final volume planned will subject to further analysis and interpretation some of the major issues of the study as a whole in their bearing on the work of the churches in social education and action.

Sincere gratitude is due to the several authors for their devotion and creativity in the writing of these volumes. In all the volumes of this series, the authors have been free to write as they wished and to accept or reject suggestions or criticisms. In the final analysis, each book is the responsibility of the writers.

Others have made valuable contributions to the total study effort of which this volume is an important part. The Reverend Cameron P. Hall, Executive Director of the Department, has given the project his unfailing and effective administrative support. Professor Howard R. Bowen, former Economic Consultant to the Study, made an invaluable contribution in the formulation of the project and aided also in criticism of the manuscripts. The Reverend A. Dudley Ward served as Director of Studies from the beginning until the fall of 1953. He carried out with imagination and efficiency his responsibilities as organizer and coordinator, and gave help also after he had left for other important work. Since September 1953 Dr. F. Ernest Johnson has been in charge of the studies. His long experience in research and education with the Federal Council, and in other connections, has made him exceptionally qualified for this service.

A Study Committee of the Department, including both lay and clerical members and representing a variety of occupations, has reviewed the program of the study at various stages. Mr. Charles H. Seaver, Editorial Consultant and Secretary of the Study Committee, has carefully edited the manuscripts and has been available consistently for counsel.

The National Council of Churches has taken no official position and assumed no responsibility regarding the content of any of the volumes. In no sense, therefore, can or should any statement in this series be regarded as an official declaration of the National Council of Churches or of any of its units.

Preface

This book, as Mr. Charles P. Taft explains in the Foreword, is one in a series of studies in ethics and economic life. It is an analysis of the major economic problems confronting agriculture particularly as they call for ethical decisions, and of farm organizations' current programs for dealing with them. The author and the specialists with whom he consulted were aware of related issues that might reasonably have been included—for example, questions arising out of the relations of farm leaders to organized labor. On balance, however, it seemed preferable to confine the study to the topics that have been dealt with in the text. The appendix written by Charles H. Seaver, which presents data on the cooperatives, supplements the author's discussion of that topic.

In an important sense this study owes its character and content to the group of advisers consulted by the author throughout the project. Social scientists, administrators, farm leaders, and theologians assisted in the development of the original plan for the study, read and criticized successive drafts of chapters, counseled on ethical and other issues, and offered insights and judgments that supplemented and enriched the author's work. At a late stage in the study chapters 11 to 16 were read by the staffs of three national farm organizations to ensure the accuracy of the statements regarding them and their positions on economic and social problems. These and other readers are, of course, in no way responsible for any opinions expressed, which are the author's own.

Some may not agree with the emphasis placed on certain facts, and the lack of emphasis on, or omission of, others. For these readers it may be helpful to explain that the author's main purposes were to present an analysis of the important social and economic problems of agriculture in terms of research findings to date; to indicate the relation of ethical values to the solution of these problems; to show how general farm organizations are working toward their solution; and to show in what ways ethically sensitive farm leaders exercise influence in helping farm groups formulate and achieve their group goals.

WALTER W. WILCOX

PART I

The Setting

1

Ethics and Economic Life

For the first time on record a high church official became Secretary of Agriculture when President Eisenhower appointed Ezra Taft Benson, an apostle of the Mormon Church, to that post in 1953. One of the Secretary's early statements on agricultural policy began: "The supreme test of any government policy, agricultural or other, should be, 'How will it affect the character, morals, and well-being of our people? . . .' It is doubtful if any man can be politically free who depends upon the State for sustenance." Many people in the months that followed attributed Secretary Benson's economic philosophy, as indicated by his public statements and policy decisions, to his religious views, and to the Christian ethical principles to which he subscribed.

Christian ethics, however, does not necessarily point to a single economic philosophy. Many clergymen agree with Secretary Benson's philosophy; yet other clergymen subscribe to an economic doctrine that favors extensive governmental programs for farming. Christian laymen are similarly divided on their approach to the solution of farm problems. Both groups may have read the same economic textbooks. Both may have observed the plight of poverty-stricken farmers and farm workers and become well acquainted with the more typical farm families and also with wealthy farmers. Yet they hold widely different ideas regarding the extent to which individual farmers require and should rely on government assistance in order to deal with their economic problems.

ECONOMIC LEGISLATION

Most of our legislation deals with economic problems. The President's legislative program for Congress in recent years is a good illustration. Expansion of the social security program, Federal assistance in housing, an improved health program, Taft-Hartley Act revisions, revisions of farm legislation, more liberal foreign trade policy, tax revision, and construction of the St. Lawrence Seaway all involve economic issues.

But it is the ethical outlook—of the legislators, of the special interest groups, and basically of the citizens—that plays the major role in determining political action in regard to economic problems. In fact, considerations of equity—the demand for fair play, the desire that each one deserve what he gets and get what he deserves— have largely shaped the rules which govern our economic life today. And equity, in the sense of "fairness or evenhanded impartiality," is taken in this study to be a basic ethical goal in our society.

Considerations of equity come into play in the following manner. Sharp conflicts of interest are encountered in relation to most social and economic problems. Some individuals, communities, and groups will gain if a proposed legislative or administrative action is taken; others will lose a part of their current economic advantages. Those expecting to gain favor the action; those expecting to lose usually oppose it. In a society as large as ours, however, the groups immediately helped or harmed may be only a small part of the total economy. The decision may lie with the disinterested.

Minority groups obtain action favorable to them in various ways. Some employ the familiar "log-rolling" practices, whereby legislators not vitally affected either way vote for measures in return for similar support on measures of particular interest to them. Party disciplinary measures also are used to secure favorable action on some issues and to defeat others. These log-rolling and party disciplinary tactics, however, are only a part of the picture. Many of those not vitally affected by the measure may act largely on the basis of equity or other ethical considerations. Minority groups such as farmers have succeeded in getting favorable legislative action over a period of years in part because of their appeal to equity considerations related to the issues presented. We might add that farmers also lose nonfarm support on issues where they cannot make a strong appeal on the basis of equity.

In a broad sense all the rules and regulations that permit us to function as a free society have been formulated with regard to equity between individuals and groups as well as with regard to their effect on individual freedom, initiative, production efficiency, and consumers' interests. Our modern economic society functions on the basis of regulations and practices which are what they are largely because of equity considerations. Much of our legislation may be sponsored primarily in order to improve the efficiency of production and exchange, such as bills designed to lower trade barriers or to develop the St. Lawrence Seaway. The particular authorizations and regulations adopted, however, involve equity considerations for the immediately affected groups.

While equity is perhaps the most important of the ethical considerations which have shaped our economic institutions, such ethical norms as honesty, truth, and productivity also have left an indelible imprint. Moreover, farm people stress certain values: neighborliness, a sense of stewardship of the resources they control, kindness to farm animals, the virtue of productive work, full utilization of resources, and the primary responsibility of the individual and the family for their own welfare with a minimum of assistance or regulation on the part of government.

COMMON SOCIAL GOALS

Individuals differ in their personal interests and goals. Yet the citizens of each country have a number of social goals which are widely shared. Some of the goals that seem to be common in the United States may be noted here.

Efficient use of resources is one of our major goals. We as a nation favor private enterprise because we believe it is the best way to get our resources used efficiently in producing the goods and services wanted by consumers. Yet of course we recognize that for equitable distribution some goods and services must be provided by government; e.g., postal service, water supply, education, highways, etc. Some believe a minimum of governmental participation and regulation is needed; others believe government participation and regulation should be more extensive.

Equality of opportunity—in relation to potential achievement—is another agreed goal. We fall short of reaching it, but our extensive public school and state-supported university system is an important part of our public effort in this direction. The 1954 Supreme Court decision declaring unconstitutional the continued segregation of white and colored children in the public schools is one of the more recent evidences that equality of opportunity is recognized as an important social goal.

Our private enterprise system, including the acquisition and inheritance of property, results in a wide variation in personal incomes. The American people, while recognizing inequalities in ability and performance, apparently disapprove of great inequalities in income. This is one of the reasons why we have a progressive income tax. We also make relief grants, pay veterans' pensions, and provide other aid to the needy from public funds to supplement private charities. The Federal government also administers an old-age pension system. There is no final agreement on how far this equalizing process should be carried or at what point it would impair individual incentive in private enterprise.

Maximum individual initiative and freedom with a maximum of equality of opportunity, which certainly belongs among our accepted goals, may seem to represent a conflicting combination; but a practical people will apply its sense of equity to adjust such conflicts.

FARM LEADERS IN THE SOCIAL PROCESS

The literature on the ethics of business and of the professions of medicine, law, and engineering is voluminous. Writings on the equity of the farmers' position in modern capitalist society and the equity of farmers' demands for "farm relief" are extensive, but writings on the ethics of farm leadership—individual and group—as revealed in social action are almost nonexistent. Yet farm leaders in recent years have been taking an increasingly active part in our social, economic, and political life.

Good business management and efficient production continue to be the major concerns of farmers. But with each passing year the social and economic order in which we live becomes more complex. The welfare of farm families is more and more determined by actions and decisions outside their farms. Farm leaders are playing an increasing role in the social processes which give rise to these decisions and actions.

For the last twenty-five years farmers have been turning more and more to government to achieve a measure of market control in the exchange of the products of their labor. With the help of government, beginning with the Federal Farm Board in 1929, farmers have held products off the market to improve prices and have restricted production of particular crops. The government also has set price floors under farm products, and used funds from tariff receipts to make surplus-removal purchases of perishable products. Today, state and national farm leaders through farm organizations, farmers' co-operatives, and political representatives exercise great influence on the social and economic affairs of our country.

Such influence of our state and national farm leaders imposes on them great social responsibility. But the exercise of leadership is not confined to state and national officers. A farm leader is one who exercises leadership with respect to the solution of farm problems. The overwhelming majority of farm leaders act in their own, local communities interpreting the problems of the day to their neighbors. When a new problem arises, neighbors turn to them for advice.

NATURE OF FARM LEADERS' RESPONSIBILITY

Every farm leader as a United States citizen shares in the formulation and achievement of national goals. Leadership in a democratic society is a generalized function rather than an activity carried on by a few individuals. In an organization, it involves the maintenance of active consideration of important issues throughout the organization from the individual members up through the elected local and state officials to the national officers, and from the national executive officer down to the individual members again. This function is one of formulating goals and initiating action. Its exercise is a two-way process with the officers maintaining an educational program for the members and the members in turn giving the officers the benefit of their wisdom and guidance. Farm leaders and farm organizations that maintain this process are likely to arrive at decisions which are the product of the entire organization. Yet within this process the unique contribution of each individual farm leader is important.

In our highly organized rural society the individual farm leader may belong to several different groups which have somewhat different goals. Let us take a farm leader in the great agricultural state of Iowa as an example. If he is located in one of the southern counties of the state, he almost surely will be a member of the local Soil Conservation Association. He may belong to a local group living in a single watershed (natural water run-off area) which has a separate watershed association. He may have sheep on his farm and be an active leader in the Iowa Sheep and Wool Growers Association. He probably is an officer in his local church and in the county Farm Bureau, the county unit in the state and national Farm Bureau Federation.

An active farm leader is looked to in his community for counsel and advice on issues which arise in local, county, state, and national groups. A number of the broader goals of these various groups are identical. Farm leaders have a responsibility for helping to formulate these common goals. They also have a responsibility for helping each of the groups in which they hold leadership positions to make progress toward these common goals. It is sheer folly, however, to assert, as is so often done, that what is good for the farmers in Willow Creek Watershed is good for Ringgold County and for the entire country. At best such statements are half-truths. Much of what is good for Willow Creek Watershed is good for the nation. But usually a specific proposal involves some advantage for the Willow Creek Watershed that is not fully shared by other groups in the county and in the economy.

At some point or points the goals or objectives of each interest group within a nation come into conflict with those of other groups. Community and economic-interest groups, such as the dairymen, organize primarily because they do have special interests not shared by others. Interests which are common to other groups usually are not stressed by the group leaders; rather, they give their attention to the special interests. These are the issues which hold the group together and make possible the mobilization of its resources. Achievement of even these special-interest goals can be attained only by education and persuasion—essential elements of leadership.

The social responsibilities of farm leaders are manifold. In addition to their role in formulating goals and initiating group action they have the task of resolving conflicts of interest within their membership. They also assume much of the burden of resolving conflicts of interests between their own and other groups in society. But the greatest social responsibility of farm and all other leaders, whether they realize it or not, is that of keeping their members aware of the more general interests and goals which all groups in the economy share. The narrower interests of the group are more fully achieved when their leaders take the initiative in keeping the members of the group aware of the interests and goals shared by others.

An analysis of economic effects gives a partial basis for reconciling conflicting interests. In rare cases the benefits of a program exceed the costs for all groups under all conditions. No conflict of interests arises in such cases, though education and persuasion are needed to achieve the desired goal. In many cases, however, costs exceed economic benefits for some groups while others receive benefits which are much greater than their costs. Farm leaders have a more difficult role in dealing with these situations. Some groups may bene- fit partially or wholly at the expense of other groups. Farm leaders will take account of the economic issues, but in the last analysis social action depends on the exercise of formal or informal political power. This brings us back to the earlier observation that, because of the large number who participate in the process of social action who are not directly affected by special-interest issues, mobilization of political power largely takes the form of organizing support or oppo- sition by dramatizing the equity and other ethical considerations involved.

Political power is not like mechanical or animal power. Social groups can arrive at rational decisions. Social groups are organized, "led," and mobilized by their leaders for the exercise of political power. Each of these leaders is the product of his physical and social heritage, possessed of reason, a conscience, and an ethical basis for judgments. For guidance leaders can use such economic analyses as are available, but to a large extent they must depend on their own analyses, on the precedents established in our cultural and economic development, and on their own ethical standards.

A Tradition of Farm Influence

In this study of social responsibility in farm leadership, a large and important sector of our economy is directly involved. During the greater part of our national history more of our people have been "gainfully employed" in farming than in all other occupations com- bined. They were a vast majority prior to the Civil War. In some states they are still a majority. And, though in the United States of 1955 hardly 10 per cent of the gainfully employed are engaged in agriculture, their production is adequate to the needs of a fast- growing population and is as important as ever to the nation's economy.

The tradition persists that the people who produce essential food and fiber, even though they are now a minority, have a right never-theless to exert a strong, collective influence in state or national government. And they do. With their organizations and leadership, not only the special problems of agriculture but also related problems of wider range are brought within the scope of discussion and action —right down at the grassroots as well as in state and national gather-ings. And they bring to a consideration of these problems resources of information and understanding that were not available a few years ago. With increased information and improved communication fa-cilities, a broader sense of social responsibility may be expected of farm leadership. Farm leaders may gain influence by including in their concern not only the problems of the particular groups they represent but also the social and economic problems of all agricultural groups. They also may be expected to be increasingly sensitive to the wel-fare of the whole economy.

2

Is Agriculture "Different"?

Farm leaders have always maintained that their problems are "different." Is this true? If so, what are the key differences which in recent years have caused farmers to turn to government to improve their equity position in the economy? Some farm leaders have maintained that farming is more important than other vocations because of the physiological requirements of the body for food in order to maintain life. Others have affirmed that farmers are the key economic group in the economy, causing the economy as a whole to prosper when they prosper and vice versa. More recent investigations indicate that in an urbanized industrial economy other vocations such as engineering, manufacturing, transportation, and public health rival food production in importance.

Certainly farmers are producers of one of the important groups of raw materials. Prices of raw materials usually fall first and farthest in a business decline and lead other prices up in a period of inflation. In this sense farm price movements often foreshadow other economic developments. But investigations have not uncovered, nor does observation disclose, any peculiar characteristics of farmers which make them more or less important than any other group in the economy which receives the same percentage (6 to 8 per cent) of the national income.

In earlier years farm leaders were often inflationists. Farmers had difficulty in paying their debts in periods of falling prices. As late as 1910, 83 per cent of the total capital invested in farming was represented by the value of farm lands and buildings. Farmers who went into debt to buy or improve farm land in prosperous years were often unable to pay off those debts because of a drop in the general price level. No other major industry except mining and petroleum production requires such a high investment in "permanent capital" in relation to the value of its annual production.

Moreover, farming is the only industry where most of the investment is on an individual or family basis. Well over half the families engaged in farming since colonial times have owned their own farms, in contrast with corporate ownership of most mines and oil wells. Miners and oil field workers work merely for wages and are but little affected by price-level declines so long as they continue to hold their jobs. With farm ownership widespread, it is no wonder that farm leaders have been the largest group of inflationists in periods of falling and depressed prices.

FARMING A BIOLOGICAL INDUSTRY

Farming does differ from most other industries because of the biological nature of its production processes. In many respects farming is as sensitive to price changes as is any other industry. There is much shifting from one product to another on this account, but the responses are delayed several weeks to several years. Broiler production can be increased or decreased within a matter of weeks. It takes about a year, however, to increase the number of laying hens on hand, and from two to three years to bring dairy heifers into milk production. An increase in market demand, which sets economic forces in motion to increase the supply of farm products, may not continue until the increased production is ready for market.

Farm prices vary widely, with small changes in supply or demand. The physical basis of the demand for food changes slowly with the increase in domestic population and with trends in food consumption habits. Families, in the aggregate, tend to spend a constant percentage of their income for food. This gives rise to changes in the amount spent for food when either unemployment or inflation occurs.

A drop in the demand for food because of general unemployment causes farm prices to fall sharply, since farmers cannot quickly cut back their production. In fact, except in a few years when severe droughts have occurred, total farm output has always been stable or on an upward trend. Supply and demand are kept in balance when the market falls by selling approximately the same quantities in the retail markets at lower prices. Since marketing and processing charges are relatively stable, moderately lower retail prices cause severe declines in farm prices. Roughly speaking, the change in either direction in farm prices is from two to two and one-half times as great as the change in retail food prices.

In periods of inflation we have the opposite of periods of unemployment, and expenditures for food rise with increases in consumers' income. Retail prices rise moderately, and farm prices rise sharply. After a period of time supplies of farm products may increase and prices decline.

An excellent example of the time required for increased production in response to increased demand occurred in the beef cattle industry from 1950 to 1953. Because of the Korean inflation retail beef and live cattle prices started to rise in 1950. The following tabulation shows the per capita disposable income, the farm price of beef cattle, and the per capita supplies of beef cattle slaughtered during the five-year period 1949-54.

Year	Per Capita Disposable Personal Income	U. S. Average Farm Price of Beef Cattle per 100 lb.	Per Capita Supplies of Beef Slaughtered (lbs. Consumed)
1949	$1,255	$19.80	63.0
1950	1,357	23.30	62.5
1951	1,458	28.70	55.2
1952	1,497	24.30	61.2
1953	1,553	16.70	75.0
1954	1,561	16.00	79.2

The first effect of the increased demand was a decline in marketings of beef cattle as farmers held back animals and built up their herds to expand output later. By the fall of 1952 the herd building phase was largely completed and market supplies of cattle increased sharply. Slaughter of cattle and calves increased 30 per cent increasing per capita supplies of beef 13.8 pounds in 1953 over 1952, and farm prices dropped sharply; market supplies increased still further in 1954 and prices continued a little lower.

On the supply or production side there is considerable variation in individual crop yields from year to year because of the weather. While annual crops such as potatoes, cabbage, or individual grains may be increased or decreased in acreage in line with economic conditions, farmers seldom let productive land lie idle, and if one crop is reduced others are increased. It is partly because of this practice of fully utilizing the land each year that the total supply of farm products maintains a relatively stable upward trend regardless of price changes.

Agricultural and Industrial Prices Contrasted

One great difference between farmers and manufacturers is in their price and production policies in a depression. The classic example occurred in the years 1929-32. During that period industrial prices dropped only 23 per cent, while manufacturers cut production 40 per cent. In contrast, farm production dropped only 3 per cent (due to weather), while farm prices declined 57 per cent.

There are several reasons for this vastly different economic behavior of farmers and manufacturers. It can be summed up by saying that farm families minimize their losses by keeping up or increasing production even though prices fall. On the other hand manufacturers' costs and markets are such that they minimize their losses by laying off workers and cutting production—measures that tend to maintain relatively stable prices.

The Race Between Output and Markets

Farm output has been increasing at a surprisingly steady rate of 2 to 3 per cent a year for several decades. In the 1930s the rate of increase dropped off because of the Great Depression and a series of drought years. Farm production took an unusual spurt, however, in the early 1940s, resulting in a level of production in 1950 as high as if the normal rate of increase had occurred throughout the 1930s (Figure 1).

As mentioned earlier, except for years of widespread drought farmers have never decreased their total production from one year to another. A series of good crop years, such as in the early 1950s at a time when foreign market outlets were declining, resulted in excessive supplies and sharp declines in market prices. Many people looking beyond the immediate future, however, expect population increases within a period of twenty to twenty-five years to be so great that farmers may find it difficult to feed the urban dwellers.

On the other hand, the increase in farm output from year to year is now equal to or in excess of our rate of increase in population. If the rate of increase in farm output continues to exceed the rate of population increase, as now seems probable, farmers are indeed in for a period of relatively low prices and incomes. We now export around 10 per cent of our farm production, largely cotton, wheat, tobacco, fats and oils, and dried fruits. The possibilities of expanding our exports at profitable prices are limited. The possibilities of increasing per capita consumption in the domestic market except at the expense of sharply lower prices are no more encouraging.

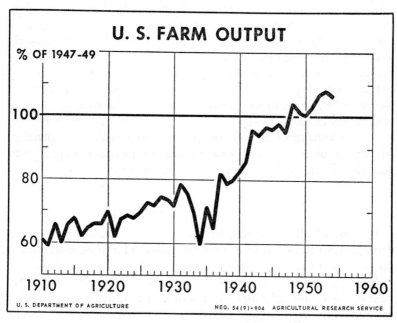

Figure 1

If, on the other hand, the rate of population increase should exceed the rate of increase in farm output, farm prices will strengthen. Under such conditions we would export less and probably draw on other parts of the world for a larger share of our food supplies.

Agriculture is different from most industries in that in many ways these two vital trends are independent of each other. This is readily seen in the case of the trend in population. The factors which will determine our future birth and death rates are numerous, and the level of output of United States farms is only one of the minor factors.

The relative independence of the upward trend in farm output requires a little more explanation. Since 1920 increases in farm output have been due almost entirely to increased yields per acre and increased production per animal. We have not increased the acreage of land cropped, yet we increased output 50 per cent, while workers on farms dropped 25 per cent. Improved technology, including improved varieties of crops and breeding stock, the substitution of tractor for horse power, and much heavier use of fertilizers, is the basis of our uptrend in the output of United States farms. Favorable farm prices cause farmers to accelerate their rate of adoption of improved technology. But, as was seen in the 1929-32 period, unfavorable prices do not cause production to decline; they merely slow down the rate of increase.

How fast will farm production increase in the future? Probably between 2 and 3 per cent per year. It will increase faster if prices are favorable, but it may continue to increase faster than our population increases, even though prices are unfavorable. Continued economic advantages in the adoption of improved production practices in periods of a cost-price squeeze lead to increased output even though net returns from farming are unsatisfactory.

Too Many Farms too Small

In spite of all our farm programs of recent years, many of our farms remain too small or too poor to provide full-time employment and sufficient income for a farm family.

In 1949, 1.2 million farms (22 per cent) accounted for 73 per cent of the farm marketings. On the other hand, in 1949, 1.5 million farm families (29 per cent) were netting less than $1000 cash income from all farm and nonfarm sources. They had little income either from farming or from nonfarm sources.

For the most part these small unproductive farms, in communities lacking nonfarm employment opportunities, are found in the Southeast. They also are found in the cut-over and hilly areas of the lake states and, in limited numbers, in every state of the Union.

Key Differences

There are many other ways in which farming differs from other occupations; length of hours worked per day and the relative isolation of the farm family, to name but two. We wish, however, to focus attention on those differences which have given rise to farmers' demands for government action to improve their economic conditions. From this point of view the key differences between agriculture and other industries are the widespread ownership of land and tools of production in agriculture, creating unusually difficult credit problems in periods of falling prices; the biological nature of the production processes which makes production adjustments slow and difficult to control; the fact that most labor cannot be dismissed in periods of falling prices, making it uneconomic to contract total output in business recessions even though sharp price declines occur; the tendency for the rate of technological improvement to exceed the rate of population increase, resulting in "burdensome" market supplies in periods of normal or favorable weather; and well over a million farms which are too small to be economic family units. These are the aspects of the agricultural industry which people have in mind particularly when they say that agriculture is "different."

3

Standards of Equity for Farm People

We have just reviewed some of the ways in which agriculture is different from other industries. We shall now examine the long-continuing and widely held view that farm people as a group have not prospered as much as other groups in our economy.

This view is based on the following claims: The per capita income of farm people is now, and for years has been, roughly half the per capita income of nonfarm people. Farm people work longer hours and live in communities with poorer schools, fewer hospitals, and fewer doctors.

Farm leaders for years have cited price and income statistics as indicative of the need for remedial governmental programs. Let us look at two of these key statistics. In 1954 the per capita income of people living on farms was $918 in contrast to an income of $1836 per capita for nonfarm people. Also in 1954 farm prices averaged 89 per cent of parity. In other words, their products had only 89 per cent as much purchasing power per unit in terms of goods and services purchased by farm families as in the base period 1910-14. Are these data valid evidence that farm people are a disadvantaged economic group?

Per Capita Income of Limited Significance

A complete answer to the above question could take us into an involved statistical inquiry. Let us rather review just a few of the key reasons why such statistics have only limited significance. The per capita income figures are clouded by a number of considerations. Farm families tend to have more children than urban families, hence, more nonworkers. Also, many families after spending their working life in urban employment retire on small suburban acreages and are counted as farmers by census takers.

Probably as many as one-third of our full-time farmers live on small or unproductive farms, produce very few crops and livestock products for the market, and have exceedingly low incomes. These low incomes when averaged with the higher incomes of the farmers who produce most of the products for commercial markets create a misleading impression. Obviously the per capita incomes of people living on the farms which produce most of the products for commercial markets are much higher than this national average. Finally, the rental value of farm housing and the value of food and fuel used by the farm family are lower than is true for urban families.

There are similar weaknesses in the income data for all nonfarm people.

Another type of income comparison is helpful. In 1949 about 2 million farms (37 per cent of the total number enumerated by the census) produced 85 per cent of all farm products sold. Their incomes averaged about the same as the incomes of urban families in 1949. Since then, however, urban incomes have increased 25 per cent or more in relation to farm incomes.

In spite of all their pitfalls, comparative income data indicate great disparity of income between the bulk of farm families and the more typical urban families, with the most serious income discrepancies occurring between full-time farm families producing little for commercial markets and the families of the employed skilled and unskilled urban workers.

PARITY PRICES EXPLAINED

The parity price ratios are even more widely used to measure the relative economic position of farmers. Parity prices are computed for each farm product by a formula designed to indicate what price would be required for it to have a purchasing power equivalent to its purchasing power in the chosen base period. Thus, a hundred bushels of wheat at full parity prices would buy as much for the farmer in terms of goods used in production and family living, interest, and taxes as in 1910-14.

Since farm prices averaged 89 per cent of parity in 1954 a given quantity of representative farm products would buy only 89 per cent as much of the nonfarm commodities and services as in the 1910-14 base period. We should not, however, jump to the conclusion that the relative position of farmers has deteriorated precisely 11 per cent.

Prices are only one of the economic variables. The volume of crops and livestock marketed, the cost of production, and the number of farm families sharing in the total farm income, all are important considerations.

Farm output has increased about 70 per cent since 1910-14; production costs per unit of output in dollars of constant purchasing power have declined. Also, the number of families engaged in farming has declined. Where does all this leave us? Are farm families today better or worse off relative to other economic groups than in the 1910-14 base period? An economist could offer his opinion, but the parity ratio of 89 per cent is not sufficient evidence in support of a specific position. Economic data cannot be marshaled to prove conclusively that farm families are either better or worse off relative to other economic groups than in 1910-14.

Usefulness of Parity Formula

The parity concept is essentially an equity concept. It has had a long political and legislative history. When the sharp drop in farm prices occurred after World War I the price indexes compiled by government agencies indicated that nonfarm prices had not fallen as much as farm prices.

Economic distress was widespread in agriculture. Farmers were in debt for land, improvements, and livestock bought at wartime price levels. Farm leaders believed that much of this economic distress was caused by the greater drop in farm prices than in nonfarm prices after the war.

George N. Peek and Hugh S. Johnson of the Moline Plow Works, Moline, Illinois, in the mid-1920s proposed a plan to equalize supply with demand on the domestic market for the export crops at a level not to exceed their fair exchange value with other commodities. They proposed to protect that value by a tariff and to export the surplus at lower world prices. The loss incurred in selling the surpluses at world prices would be absorbed by the producers on a pro rata basis. This plan was popularized under the slogan "equality for agriculture."

Many people believed that the protective tariffs on manufactured goods were largely responsible for the stability of industrial prices at relatively high levels as compared with sagging farm prices. They looked upon these proposals as a means of making the tariff effective for agriculture. This plan, developed by Peek, Johnson, and others, after considerable polishing became the McNary-Haugen Bill which twice passed Congress in 1927 and 1928 only to be vetoed both times by President Coolidge.

The early use of the slogan "equality for agriculture" in the 1920s covered two fundamental goals. The first goal was to give farmers equality of tariff protection, or insulation from world prices, with manufacturers and industrial workers. The second, which was expected to result from attainment of the first goal, was the equality of farm and nonfarm price levels in terms of prewar relationships.

As the years went by and farm leaders failed in their attempt to get the McNary-Haugen proposals enacted into law, more and more attention centered on the disparity between indexes of farm and nonfarm prices using the prewar years 1910-14 as a base. The disparity in the level of these price indexes in the 1920s became the widely accepted evidence that agriculture was "ill" and needed some "doctoring."

After a decade of public discussion of this "disparity" of farm and nonfarm prices, it was only natural that the Agricultural Act of 1933 should have as one of its major objectives to "reestablish prices to farmers at a level that will give agricultural commodities a purchasing power with respect to articles that farmers buy equivalent to the purchasing power of agricultural commodities in the base period." This objective was spelled out more precisely in subsequent agricultural acts. The 1936 Agricultural Act included the achievement of parity incomes as one of its goals, but this idea never received wide public acceptance. Obviously, from an equity standpoint, the ratio of per capita incomes of farm and nonfarm people in recent years as compared with an earlier period would be more indicative of changes in their relative economic welfare than would changes in price ratios.

The per capita income of farm people is affected by their output per person as well as by the prices received. Similarly, the per capita income of nonfarm workers is affected by output per person as well as by nonfarm price levels. While parity of incomes may represent an improvement over parity of prices as a goal, it does have certain drawbacks. For example, output per worker may have increased more for nonfarm than for farm workers, yet the increased output was achieved by heavier investments in machinery and equipment in nonfarm production. Hence a part of the increased per capita income of nonfarm people would be needed to offset extra capital investments. Another difficulty arose when attempts were made to develop specific farm programs for per capita income improvement. Administrators were unable to develop satisfactory plans for translating this over-all objective into specific commodity programs.

Since 1936 the general trend has been in the direction of incorporating specific parity price formulas in legislation. Base periods for individual commodities have been changed to give them more favorable parity prices. Specific procedures for maintaining prices at as high a percentage of parity as possible have dominated all recent general farm legislative actions. Equality or parity for agriculture has been a unifying slogan for agricultural leaders for thirty years or more. The disparity in farm and nonfarm price indexes has been the key evidence used to document this slogan. The wide appeal of this slogan should not blind us, however, to the fact that equality for agriculture cannot be fully measured by one set of price indexes no matter how inclusive they are.

OTHER APPROACHES IN DETERMINING EQUITY

What can farm leaders use if they cannot depend on the parity price ratio as a measure of the relative advantage or disadvantage of farm groups? Farm leaders in their public relations have great need for simple informative criteria in this field.

Unfortunately, broad generalizations on the basis of a few easily explained data often conceal more variations than they reveal. In view of the wide variations in income and living conditions both within agriculture and among nonfarm families, it is much more fruitful to make income or living-standard comparisons between specific groups of farm families and specific groups of nonfarm families.

Income per worker, debt position, number of modern appliances used in the home, and educational attainments of the children are some of the more important criteria which are useful in comparing the economic position of one group with another.

BASIC REASONS FOR LOW WORKER INCOMES IN AGRICULTURE

Recent studies indicate that income per farm worker (operators, family, and hired workers) compares favorably with income per nonfarm worker in the northern and western states. In the southern states, the Appalachian Highlands, and on the smaller, less productive farms in the northern and western states, income per farm worker falls below the average income of nonfarm workers.

Farm leaders should remember that there is a basic economic reason for the continued lower incomes of farm workers as a group as compared with nonfarm workers. With increased mechanization fewer workers are needed from year to year. On the other hand, there are almost twice as many farm boys reaching working age each year as there are vacancies in the farm labor force (including farm operators) due to retirement and death.

This continuing excess of farm labor relative to job opportunities makes for low returns to farm labor, which in turn encourage migration to the higher paying nonfarm jobs. Farm leaders should expect a continuing wage differential. It is an essential economic motivation for migration.

The important question is whether worker income differentials are more than sufficient to offset costs of migration. The same question applies to worker income differentials between different areas in the United States. Worker income differentials between some groups of farm and nonfarm workers and between some communities are obviously greater than would offset costs of migration.

Where such situations exist our economic system is not functioning as efficiently as it should be, and the result is inequities in income and living standards.

It is fortunate, from the standpoint of getting agreement on remedial measures, that most of our cases of inequitably low farm incomes also are cases of inefficient, low production. Farm leaders have a great challenge and opportunity in the field of improving the use of equity criteria and standards. Much improvement is needed in the identification of smaller groups within agriculture and the application of welfare criteria to them.

Our society is not static. The position of groups within agriculture and of specific rural communities is subject to continual change. Each farm leader must keep under constant review all the social and economic measures which throw light on the position of the group in which he is interested. It is his responsibility to keep the group informed regarding all the relevant criteria. But the greatest leadership talents are required in guiding group thinking and action when the group becomes aware that it is in a disadvantaged position. This is true also when a group becomes interested in another disadvantaged group. What action should be taken to correct the situation? Obviously corrective action should be based on an understanding of what social and economic conditions gave rise to the disadvantages found. Farm leaders play one of their most significant roles in helping groups understand the social and economic conditions which have given rise to such inequities as exist from time to time in our society.

4

How Much Price Stabilization Is Desirable?

The central aim of all farm price-stabilization programs is to prevent farm prices from fluctuating as widely as under free market conditions. Thus farm income is stabilized or increased somewhat in periods when it would otherwise be low due to falling farm prices. This chapter reviews briefly the results of price-stabilization programs, makes an evaluation of them insofar as possible, and presents the important considerations regarding several of the critical issues involved in current farm price-support controversies.

Farm price-stabilization programs in operation at the present time are of three types. First, and by far the most important, are the mandatory price-support programs for the basic and designated nonbasic commodities. The basic commodities specified by legislation are corn, cotton, wheat, rice, tobacco, and peanuts. The designated nonbasics are milk used for manufacturing, butterfat, honey, tung nuts, and wool. Prices are supported by government loans and by direct government purchases, except in the case of wool. In that case direct payments are made to the wool producers based on the difference between the seasonal average price received by producers and the announced government support price.

Second, the prices of all other products may be supported at levels up to 90 per cent of parity at the discretion of the Secretary of Agriculture to the extent that funds are available and conditions of equity between the support levels of different commodities are met. The Secretary also has available to him each year 30 per cent of the customs (tariff) receipts, which may be used for making surplus-removal purchases when individual commodities are suffering from excessive supplies in relation to market outlets. These latter funds are used to assist in the orderly marketing of perishable products, while loans are used primarily to stabilize prices of the storable products. Products bought under surplus-removal programs are donated to school lunch programs and charitable and public institutions.

Third, marketing agreements together with marketing orders are used to regulate the marketing of specified fruits and vegetables in twenty to thirty areas, and the marketing of fluid milk in about fifty of the larger urban milk markets. Each of these marketing agreements and orders was adopted after a favorable vote by the producers supplying the particular market. These orders, issued by the Secretary of Agriculture in accord with the Marketing Agreement legislation of 1937, as amended, are in effect marketing regulations.

In the case of fruits and vegetables, the orders usually relate to grade and size of product which may be marketed. Producers in effect ask the Secretary of Agriculture to issue orders limiting the marketing of inferior grades of a product in the interest of increasing the market returns for the entire crop. In the case of urban milk markets, the marketing orders provide a formula for the determination of producers' prices and specify a number of practices which must be followed by producer and distributor groups in their marketing operations.

The origins of the government price-supporting loans for storable farm products are found in the price-stabilization operations for wheat and cotton of the Federal Farm Board, 1930-31. Price-supporting loans have been available each year since 1933. The authorization to use 30 per cent of the customs receipts for surplus-removal purchases was granted in an amendment (Section 32) to the Agricultural Adjustment Act in 1935. California, in particular, had had favorable experience with marketing agreement or market prorate legislation in the late 1920s. Largely on the basis of this experience, authority for entering into marketing agreements and issuing marketing orders was included in the broad Agricultural Adjustment Act in 1933. This legislation was substantially modified and strengthened in 1937.

Have these stabilization programs in fact stabilized farm prices? A review of the behavior of all farm prices and the prices of individual products since 1933 indicates that these programs have had a modest stabilizing influence. Supplies of corn and cotton, which accumulated under the price-supporting loans in 1933, were utilized in 1934 to offset shortages caused by drought. Supplies of grains and cotton under loan had reached almost embarrassing proportions in 1939 when World War II broke out, and these stocks turned out to be blessings in disguise.

Stocks accumulated under price-support loans again in 1948 and 1949 and were helpful in holding down the 1951 and 1952 Korean inflationary boom. By 1954, however, stocks had become excessive again. They were large in relation both to prudent reserves and to commercial requirements. Their orderly reduction constitutes one of the serious problems associated with continued price-stabilization programs.

An important consideration in evaluating the extent to which price-stabilization measures have stabilized farm prices is the trend in the general price level since 1933. Both the general price level and prices of farm products have been on an uptrend almost continuously. Price-stabilization measures work most effectively under such conditions; the general price level is often higher when stored products are returned to the market than it was at the time of removal. It is largely because of this situation that the government realized a net profit on its cotton stabilization operations from 1933 through 1953.

Without question, the price-supporting loans for storable products and the marketing orders in the fluid-milk markets have been the most effective. The surplus-removal operations utilizing Section 32 funds (from customs receipts) have been much more limited in coverage and application but have had important stabilizing effects for a number of the perishable products.

Has this added stability in farm prices been worth its cost? This is a far more difficult question to answer. In reality, it is several questions. How much have the programs cost the government? Have the control programs associated with the price supports contributed to inefficiency in production? How much have the programs increased the cost of food to consumers? To what extent were higher and more stable prices for some products achieved at the expense of lower and more unstable prices for other farm products? How serious is the conflict between our domestic farm price-support activity and our policy of promoting freer international trade? If we take these questions one at a time, we can get a much better understanding of the costs relative to the benefits of the price-stabilization programs.

GOVERNMENT COSTS

The cost of all price-support programs, including administrative costs, Commodity Credit Corporation losses, Section 32 expenditures for surplus-removal purchases, and export programs such as the International Wheat Agreement, 1933 to June 30, 1953, aggregated 3.8 billion dollars. This compares with a total value of crops and livestock marketed during this period of 335 billion dollars.

When viewed in this over-all way, stabilization costs of one to two per cent of the value of products marketed do not appear to be excessive. Costs as low as this would appear to be justified even though the stabilization accomplishment has been modest. Costs could have been kept even lower, however, if specific price supports such as those for potatoes and eggs had been revised or discontinued earlier.

Those familiar with the farm price supports over a period of years may remember the overproduction associated with the potato price support program from 1947 to 1950. The cost of surplus-removal programs and C.C.C. losses on potatoes during this period totaled $584,114,068. Surely the potato price stabilization costs were excessive in relation to accomplishments. This also was true for several other commodities such as eggs and flaxseed. It would be impossible, however, to determine precisely how much the total government costs could have been reduced without reducing effective stabilization activities.

EFFECT ON EFFICIENCY

The question of the effect of the programs on the efficiency of farming operations is somewhat more complicated. Where acreage allotments have been used to restrict production, their direct effect in many cases has been to reduce efficiency. Allotments are distributed largely on the basis of past history. This prevents normal shifts in acreage from taking place. Farmers have to break up their rotations and subdivide their fields to plant within their allotments. The reduction in acreage is brought about by a roughly equal reduction in allotments both on the most productive and on the least productive land. Often individual farm families cannot fully utilize their available labor and equipment when complying with allotments.

But offsetting these direct effects are a number of indirect adjustments resulting from price stabilization programs. Many farmers had been planting larger acreages of cultivated crops than they could care for properly, or than their land would grow without excessive depletion and erosion losses. A restrictive acreage allotment on such farms increased land and labor efficiency. This was especially true in the early years of the crop-control programs.

The price-stabilization programs had another important influence on efficiency. Farm output has increased almost 50 per cent during the period these price-stabilization programs have been in effect. This increased output has been accomplished with 25 per cent less labor. Output per hour of farm labor has increased approximately 100 per cent since 1933. The reduction in income uncertainty (assurance of more stable prices) as a result of government price-stabilization programs caused farmers to speed up their rate of adoption of improved farming practices and make larger labor-saving capital investments.

When all aspects of this question are considered, it seems probable that the net effect of the programs to date has been an increase in farming efficiency.

Effect on Consumers' Prices

Contrary to public opinion, price-stabilization programs have probably increased the food supplies and lowered food costs of urban people. Lower prices come about in this way: We pointed out how the increased stability of income contributed to the sharp increase in output mentioned earlier. This larger output than would have occurred in the absence of stabilization programs has kept prices to consumers from increasing even further in recent years.

People often call attention to the restriction programs for specific products such as wheat and cotton, but forget that the diverted acreages are used for other crops and for soil conservation purposes. Surplus-removal purchases, to the surprise of many people, often have had the effect of increasing the amount of a perishable product harvested and marketed. Many times unusually favorable yields of particular fruits and vegetables expand supplies in relation to immediate market outlets to the extent that market prices fail to cover harvesting costs. When this happens a part of the crop is left unharvested. A surplus-disposal program that purchases a part of the supplies for distribution for school lunches and to charitable institutions in effect increases the total supplies of such products which reach consumers.

These summary statements hold true even though many specific price-stabilization activities resulted in a reduction in consumers' supplies and in some price increases at the time they were in operation. One of the surprising conclusions reached by a group of economists who studied the effects of price supports on potato prices and production was that the government-guaranteed prices were lower than prices which would have prevailed in the markets during those years in the absence of price supports. Potato producers responded to the lower guaranteed price with so much enthusiasm that even at the lower prices the government was forced to purchase and destroy substantial quantities of potatoes in order to keep its price guarantees. The government price-support program for potatoes resulted in larger consumer supplies and lower prices during those years than would have prevailed under normal supply and demand conditions.

In spite of these results, the potato price-support program was discontinued because of the continued excessive production in response to the guaranteed prices. The public quite rightly objected to the destruction of a part of the potato crop each year and the high government cost of the program.

ADVERSE EFFECTS ON PRODUCERS OF NONBASIC PRODUCTS

We come now to a consideration of the effect of the price-support and production-control measures on producers of nonsupported products. Poultrymen, dairymen, and beef-cattle feeders, who buy their feed, believe that they are at a disadvantage when price supports hold feed grains at prices above free market levels. Established vegetable growers also may be hurt by the shift of a part of the acreage taken out of a price-supported crop to the production of their specialty. The extra acreage grown may result in overproduction and sharply lower prices for their vegetable crops. Dairymen and beef-cattle producers also complain that acreage restrictions on the basic crops result in increased acreages of forages and pastures and in an expansion of dairy and beef production.

Unquestionably, the question of using or restricting the use of diverted acres is one of the major equity issues associated with price-stabilization and control programs. Corn, cotton, and wheat normally occupy almost half, or 160 to 170 million acres, of our crop land. A reduction of 12 to 15 per cent in their acreage frees 20 to 25 million acres for other uses. Farmers who do not produce the basic or designated nonbasic crops fail to get substantial benefits and may suffer losses from the operation of production-control programs as indicated above. The use of Section 32 funds to make surplus-removal purchases of these other products when supplies force prices down sharply helps to a limited extent, but the basic fact remains that the free use of diverted acres may result in serious inequities. This problem will be discussed more fully later.

On the other hand, complaints that price supports on feed grains cause hardships for the feed-using livestock industries are based on short-run effects only. Livestock producers complain when the support program results in higher than free market prices of feed grains, but conveniently forget the periods when the opposite has been true. Price-stabilization programs have been successful in removing part of the instability from feed grain prices and supplies. This has had a stabilizing effect on the livestock industries and in a long-run setting is an important improvement for most livestock producers.

Price Stabilization and International Trade

Farm stabilization programs at times hold domestic prices above world price levels. In the case of export crops such as wheat and cotton, the government must subsidize export sales in foreign markets at such times or we fail to continue normal exports. Import quotas or other restrictions also must be imposed, or the higher domestic price levels will attract imports in sufficient quantities to defeat the price-stabilization program.

Government restrictions on imports and assistance on exports interfere with our objectives of promoting freer international trade. Thus far we have found no means of resolving these conflicts. For the most part we have said that more stable domestic prices are our first objective. But this has not always been true. The decisions whether or not to impose additional trade restrictions in order to maintain domestic prices at desired levels are always difficult to make. So far we have not found any politically acceptable method for minimizing this conflict. Restrictions on imports, in particular, have been increased in recent years to protect our domestic price-support programs. This continued interference with the attainment of our goal of freer international trade continues to be one of the important costs involved in maintaining domestic price-stabilization programs.

SOME CRITICAL CURRENT ISSUES

Government farm price-stabilization activities probably have become a permanent part of our economic system. Those who would abolish all these programs are in a distinct minority. Farm leaders find there is widespread disagreement, however, on:

1. The level of supports that should be maintained in relation to "long-run normal" free market prices.

2. The number of commodities that should be included in the group having mandatory supports.

3. The restrictions that should be placed on the use of diverted acres when marketing quotas and acreage allotments are in effect.

4. The resolution of the conflict between domestic price stabilization and freer international trade.

5. The distribution of benefits among farm families.

Both farm and nonfarm people take different positions on these questions, largely because of lack of information or disagreement regarding the economic consequences of alternative lines of action. They also may hold different views as to what is equitable both between groups in agriculture and between farm and nonfarm groups. A third factor which is often mentioned in popular discussions of alternatives is their effect on individual farmers' freedom.

Farm leaders' responsibilities in this field take many forms. Surely the major responsibility is to increase understanding. Farm leaders themselves range from fully informed honest individuals to poorly informed persons and outright demagogues. Economic relationships in these fields are far more complex than the simple supply-demand relationships taught in our schools and colleges. So-called expert advice may be conflicting, for many trained economists fail to study the situations that prevail at specific times and places and arrive at erroneous conclusions based on "general economic principles."

Increased general understanding of the consequences of farm price-stabilization programs requires continued study of all aspects of the problem with an open mind. This is true for trained economists as well as for farm leaders. In addition it requires continuing and aggressive leadership activity to acquaint both farm and nonfarm groups with the results of these studies. We cannot expect to have full agreement on what facts are relevant and on the interpretation of their significance. We can expect, however, a severalfold increase in the areas of agreement as a result of being better informed.

More Economic Analyses Needed

Each individual price-stabilization activity requires study. Who will benefit? How much will they benefit? Who will be placed at a disadvantage? Will the welfare position of the economy as a whole be increased or decreased? All too often we make our political decisions, whether or not to adopt specific stabilization measures, on the basis of political symbols or attractive catchwords rather than on the basis of economic analysis.

It has been said that President Eisenhower's farm message to Congress in January 1954 was preceded by the most comprehensive and widespread study of desirable policies for agriculture ever undertaken. Without disagreeing with this statement, one who has seen the results of these studies in the form of group reports and resolutions must conclude that much more in the way of general understanding of economic consequences of particular stabilization measures is badly needed. Groups are usually correct in their conclusions regarding the short-run economic consequences of a specific stabilization measure for themselves. They are often incorrect in their evaluation of its long-run effect on themselves and in their calculation of its effect on other groups in the economy. It is too much to expect all members in a group to become fully informed on these complex economic issues; it is not too much to expect their leaders to improve their present level of economic understanding.

No final conclusion has been reached either as to the level of support of individual commodities or as to the particular commodities to be included in government price-support programs. While the recent trend has been toward lower government price supports and supports on fewer commodities, this trend may be reversed at any time if a majority of farmers and others conclude that the gains of increased stabilization measures would more than offset the costs.

Experience with the Agricultural Act of 1954 will give us additional badly needed information on the effectiveness of lowering support prices on basic commodities, which is a highly controversial issue at the present time.

FREEDOM *vs.* SECURITY

Contemporary discussions commonly include statements to the effect that the basic issue posed by price stabilization programs is the choice between security and freedom. Secretary Benson, soon after he took office in January 1953, issued an official policy statement in which he said:

Freedom is a God-given, eternal principle vouchsafed to us under the Constitution. It must be continually guarded as something more precious than life itself. . . . It is generally agreed that there is undue concentration of power in the Federal Government. . . . Individual freedom and citizen responsibility depend upon the principle of helping the individual help himself. . . . In the administration of this Department, the guiding purpose will be to strengthen the individual integrity, freedom, and the very moral fiber of each citizen. . . .

The word "freedom" has been given a special meaning in this statement; namely, freedom from governmental direction or interference. The ethical issue involved in price-stabilization programs, however, is not the simple choice between more security and more freedom. Security itself involves freedom from other external forces that may be viewed as more limiting to individual initiative than is the specific governmental intervention. And some farm leaders say they believe farmers prefer freedom from want to freedom from governmental interference.

A keen student of ethical issues recently pointed out that Americans usually consider freedom as synonymous with liberty in the sense of absence of restraints. This is the usage customary in farm price-support discussions. He holds that in a philosophical and theological setting the full meaning of freedom must be much more than liberty, much more than freedom from regulation. In addition to the liberty people crave, there must be order, for absence of order is chaos. Real freedom for an individual in society can be achieved only by social organization, by social order.

Members of the advisory group assisting the author on this project made a number of pertinent comments on this issue, such as this: "To secure a proper degree of freedom for all people the government does have to take a hand because it is freedom of whom to do what." Another responded: "I feel that it is easy for government action to override certain other values which are, in the long run, essential to human sensitiveness to freedom itself. When government does something for people it does something to people." A little later another member joined in the discussion with the observation: "Almost always legislation which expands the freedom of one group restricts the freedom of another."

Farm leaders and farm groups are not faced with a simple choice between more freedom and more security. Viewing farm price-stabilization programs as posing a dilemma of freedom versus security is a carry-over of the pioneer habit of defining freedom negatively as the mere absence of political interference. In pioneer days the free market was such a great improvement over feudal regulations that individual "freedom" or liberty was closely identified with the absence of political interference with free markets. In our modern highly industrialized society this may or may not be true. The current issue of freedom versus security as applied to levels of price support is largely an issue of whether or not the restrictions on individual economic actions associated with particular price-stabilization measures are excessive in relation to the total or long-run economic advantages gained. Again, a resolution of this issue with respect to a particular stabilization measure requires an accurate appraisal of both the restrictions involved and the economic advantages gained.

In this connection the Evanston Assembly of the World Council of Churches, in one of its sectional reports, stated: "While the state is sometimes the enemy of freedom, under many circumstances the state is the only instrument which can make freedom possible for large sectors of the population."[1]

RESTRICTIONS ON THE USE OF DIVERTED ACRES

Earlier we described the equity problems created by the adverse effects of price supports and acreage restrictions on producers of nonsupported products. The critical current issue in the field is

[1] *The Evanston Report: The Second Assembly of the World Council of Churches*, 1954, ed. by W. A. Visser t'Hooft (New York: Harper & Brothers, 1955), p. 116.

concerned with appropriate restrictions on the use of diverted acres. It cannot be disposed of by insisting that all land taken out of price-supported crops should be kept idle or used for soil-building purposes. In the absence of a price-support and acreage-allotment program market price relationships would have prompted some shift from the acreage-allotment crop to others. On the other hand, acreage restrictions on particular crops usually are in effect in years when the prices of most nongovernment-supported crops are sagging. Producers of the price-supported crops are getting special assistance from the government. Producers of nonsupported crops insist that it is highly inequitable to give direct assistance in the form of price supports to the producers of a few crops and then allow acreages diverted from these crops under an acreage-allotment program to be planted to the nonsupported crops.

There is no final solution to the problem. The decision in recent years not to impose restrictions on the use of diverted acres has been made largely on the basis of currently important considerations of equity to needy farmers and the general welfare. In view of the widespread droughts, feed stocks were low in some areas and individual farm families who suffered drought losses urgently needed maximum production from every acre to assist in recouping their losses. Just as both general welfare and equity considerations have been weighed in reaching a decision on appropriate restrictions in recent years, a decision will have to be made each crop year based on these two criteria.

Domestic Price Stabilization *vs.* Freer Trade

We have already pointed out how farm price-stabilization programs come into conflict with our goals of freer trade. Farmers are divided among themselves on which of these goals they should put first. In addition, many nonfarm groups believe that farm price-stabilization programs are hurting the general economy more than they are helping it, primarily because of this conflict with freer trade goals. Thus far, in majority votes, domestic price-stabilization programs have been given preference and international trade regulations have been modified as necessary to permit the stabilization programs to operate effectively. This policy has resulted in the use of subsidies to maintain exports and the imposition of import controls to prevent excessive imports of price-supported commodities.

These actions are undeniable interferences with free private trading. On the other hand, the evidence indicates that, in general, subsidies are employed only to maintain "normal" exports, and import quotas are imposed only to prevent "abnormal" imports. In other words, the interferences with free private trading are limited to actions designed to reestablish the status which existed before the domestic price-support program was undertaken. Viewed in this light, domestic price-support programs have not resulted in many hardships and actually may have benefited producers in other countries. They probably have resulted in smaller exports and higher world prices of the price-supported crops such as cotton. However, the "freer traders" insist that trade restrictions to offset domestic price-support programs have a farther-reaching effect. They introduce uncertainties into international trading relations which stifle private trading. Equally well-informed farm leaders will continue to differ sharply on this issue. It is probable that compromises will continue to be made in this area which are more or less unsatisfactory to all concerned, yet which will continue to reflect the importance of these conflicting goals.

DISTRIBUTION OF BENEFITS AMONG FARM FAMILIES

Farm price-stabilization measures are considered primarily as supplements to the free market system designed to make it function more equitably in rewarding those who engage in farm production. They are not welfare measures for the redistribution of farm income on the basis of family needs. Price-stabilization measures are of little benefit to the 1.6 million full-time farm families with sales of less than $2500. This is true even though several hundred thousand sharecropper families (families who produce cotton and tobacco for a share of the crop) get some benefit from price-support programs. Their crop income per family is so low, usually $700 to $1800, that a 10 to 20 per cent improvement from price-support programs, while important, is relatively small.

The effects of price-stabilization measures differ also as between the medium-size and the larger farms. The larger farms benefit more than the medium-size farms from the reduction in income uncertainty. To the extent that subsidies are involved, the large farms benefit more, of course, on the basis of volume of business than the medium-size farms. As a part of the widespread desire to promote family farming and to prevent government policies from assisting larger than family farms, proposals have been made from time to time to set limits on the price-stabilization benefits receivable by very large farms.

From time to time small farms have been given favorable treatment in establishing acreage allotments and in computing acreage-adjustment payments. Agricultural conservation payments have always had a maximum limit although it has been changed from time to time. Proposals have been put forward for limiting price support to a fixed maximum volume of output, regardless of the total production of the largest farms. Thus far administrative problems involved in limiting the benefits for large farms have loomed larger than the anticipated benefits.

Supplementary special educational, credit, and technical assistance programs for the smaller farms which benefit little from price-support programs appear to be more feasible and desirable than attempting to exclude the large farms from price-stabilization programs.

SUMMARY

In summary, price-stabilization measures as they have been administered to date have stabilized farm prices and incomes to a limited extent and have had a small net stabilizing influence on the economy. In an over-all sense they have contributed to increased farm output.

In spite of these benefits of past programs, there is widespread disagreement today on the economic effects of specific price-stabilization measures, especially as to the level of price supports on storable crops. There is widespread disagreement also on the equity of maintaining price supports on specific commodities and not on others, and on the regulations which should govern the use of acreages diverted from the price-supported crops by acreage allotments. Disagreement continues also on how best to minimize the conflict between domestic price stabilization and freer trade goals.

Unfortunately, much of the discussion resulting from these disagreements has added more heat than light. Political symbols have been employed all too effectively as a substitute for economic information.

Farm leaders urgently need more economic information on the probable effects of specific levels of support and on other aspects of the price-support program. The issue now popularly called freedom versus security, insofar as it is applied to alternative price-stabilization measures, turns out on analysis to be largely an economic issue: Is the added stability of prices and income worth the cost in terms of required restrictions on plantings and marketings?

5

Should We Continue to Produce Surpluses to Be Given Away Abroad?

Farm leaders are troubled by the widespread hunger and need in the world, while "surpluses" accumulate at home. One of the common recommendations made to Congressional committees concerning farm legislation in recent years has been to keep price supports at relatively high levels and use any surpluses which may accumulate to feed and clothe the needy in friendly foreign countries. Why shouldn't American farmers maintain maximum production and, if available markets will not absorb the output at stable prices, why not donate the balance to undernourished and poorly clothed people in other parts of the world?

People who make these suggestions seldom consider all aspects of the problem. If we are really concerned about the needy in other countries, what are we prepared to do for them when no surpluses exist? Would welfare and equity in the world really be promoted by maintaining relatively favorable farm prices in the United States and giving away in foreign countries any surpluses that accumulate?

ECONOMIC CONSIDERATIONS

In order to get a better basis for answering these questions we need a brief review of the operation of economic forces in agriculture. Economists are quite explicit as to how our resources, land, labor, management, and capital, should be employed and rewarded in order to maximize the total output of society at any particular time. Each acre of land, each worker, each machine, and each hundred dollars in working capital should be employed in the production process where it will contribute most. Resources should be used in such a way that they produce the maximum possible. Also, each category of productive resources—labor, management, land, and capital—should be rewarded in proportion to its contribution to the total product.

The most effective way to organize the productive resources in a free enterprise economy is to reward the factors of production on the basis of their respective contributions in the productive process. Businessmen in a freely competitive economy who offer the highest rewards obtain the resources required in their undertakings. Resources are economized and channeled into the most productive uses in this way. Inefficient businessmen and production undertakings which do not yield a high value of output in relation to resource use cannot survive the competition of the more efficient. This is the economic argument.

This reasoning suggests that an agricultural policy which holds farm prices above free market prices and accumulates surpluses causes resources to be used in farming that otherwise would be producing other things of more value to society. Does this in fact happen in real life? The "real-life" complications include the influence of stability of income on technological progress and the effects of increased income on migration out of farming.

Technical progress in agriculture in recent years has been more rapid than in any earlier period in history. The relatively high price levels of the war and early postwar years and the continuing assurance of government price supports on many farm products have contributed to this progress. The assurance of relatively stable incomes has encouraged farmers to make labor-saving and output-increasing investments more rapidly than would be prudent under free market conditions. Both the availability of labor-saving machinery and the increased income in farm homes have made it easier for families to help those of their children who desired to leave home in search of other job opportunities.

Price supports which stabilize farm prices and incomes over a period of several years may result in an increase in total output and consumption in our economy, even though a part of the increased output is given away to needy people in other lands.

Some farm leaders in recent years have urged that we develop policies that are really adequate for an "economy of abundance" without specifying precisely what they mean by an economy of abundance. They imply that such policies would permit a higher level of production and distribute a larger volume of goods than are being produced currently and sold through commercial markets. What the advocates of new policies for an "economy of abundance" may be overlooking is the fact that our present private enterprise system results in the greatest per capita abundance in history.

Having chronic surpluses in some fields such as agriculture while we are still in need of other goods and services, such as better housing for low-income families and more and better public schools and roads, means that we as a nation would have a greater abundance of things we want if the labor and capital used to produce agricultural surpluses were shifted to some of these other lines of production. A little reflection indicates that a true "economy of abundance" is an economy with all workers, land, and capital employed in such a way that the value of the total product is at a maximum. This ideal cannot be realized if a part of our agricultural resources are employed to produce continuing "surpluses" which must be given away in foreign lands.

In the light of past experience it is probable that assured prices for farm output in an otherwise free market over a period of years will result in somewhat larger output than would be realized under free market prices. Hence, if "surpluses" are to be kept small in relation to total farm output, farm price supports must be kept at levels not far different from free market prices.

Farm leaders aware of the great productivity of American agriculture and of the economic difficulties involved in postwar adjustments to available markets would be happy if farmers could continue current levels of production and channel any market surpluses in this country to hungry peoples in other countries. Under circumstances now existing it is easy to "rationalize" to the effect that the welfare of the free nations would be improved if American farmers were encouraged to continue to produce in excess of market demands and the surpluses were distributed to the needy people abroad.

But this line of thinking overlooks the fact that both within our own country and elsewhere in the world needy people can be helped in the long run only by creating conditions that permit them to meet their needs through their own efforts. Charity in the form of gifts of food and fiber can have only a limited place in programs to improve the welfare of the millions who now have inadequate food and clothing year after year.

WELFARE CONSIDERATIONS

One may ask: Have the people in the United States shared their food and fiber generously in the past? Have we lived up to the highest ethical standards in past years? Undoubtedly not.

There is another side of the coin, however. A social order in which a part of the people continuously exist on charitable gifts from the more fortunate and the more industrious is unstable. Gifts, if they are not to be debasing, except in emergencies must be integrated with an appropriate self-rehabilitation program.

Yet people are starving today in many parts of the world, and gifts of our abundant food and fiber in these cases would alleviate real suffering. What are the social responsibilities of farm leaders in these circumstances? Clearly they go beyond the mere sharing of existing stocks.

When famine strikes, as in Pakistan in 1953, we do not hesitate to provide food to the starving people which they could not purchase through the commercial markets. The Marshall Plan and subsequent foreign aid programs of the United States have been the greatest international peacetime undertakings along this line. But the Marshall Plan and other foreign aid programs were not undertaken because of welfare considerations alone. We believed that economic recovery on the part of our allies was essential for our own interests. The foreign aid programs in recent years have been primarily the result of "enlightened self-interest."

How much farther should we go? Have we already gone too far? To what extent should we share our abundant production with others?

Two criteria may be used to evaluate proposals for sharing our abundant production. The first is partly a negative test. A more nearly equal or an equitable income distribution is normally a goal for a democracy or in a world of democracies. Policies designed to reduce extreme inequalities in income are favored insofar as they do not reduce production incentives, or give rise to other adverse economic consequences, or create moral dilemmas. The second test is more positive. Will the policy and program reduce group tensions and increase intergroup and international cooperation? In short, does the program appear to be fair and equitable to those who must give up a part of their income as well as to those who directly benefit?

With these two tests in mind it becomes possible for the farm leader to reach a decision on specific issues in this field. Are the price policies which give rise to surpluses of such nature that the surpluses will continue indefinitely? If they are, it is probable that a part of our resources used in creating these surpluses should be shifted to some other line of production. Furthermore it is probable that the recipients of continued gifts of food would experience greater social degradation than progress.

Recent studies and discussions indicate that United States surpluses under some circumstances might well be thus used to help finance economic expansion in underdeveloped countries. Where arrangements can be made on such a basis, surpluses might be used to play a vital role in speeding economic progress around the world.

Technical aid, which has been the bulk of our foreign aid program (other than military) in recent years, stands on a different footing. Where the aid is not used for direct consumption but for increasing the size and efficiency of a nation's productive plant, enormous benefits may accrue over a period of years. Technical aid in improving food production techniques in underdeveloped countries has made a good beginning. But the accomplishment to date should be considered only as a small start on a large and fruitful undertaking. The Western world must continually ask itself whether it is doing all that can be done effectively in this field.

We must always be alert to the needs of our international neighbors. We must continually review the functioning of our international economic system to make sure that it provides equality of opportunity for the diverse groups in the world, especially with respect to their obtaining the essential technical know-how and access to capital with which to improve themselves. We cannot wait until surpluses arise and then look around for places to dispose of them.

6

What Can Be Done About the Low-Income Problem in Agriculture?

Within the last twenty years we have made an important discovery. We find that we can understand agriculture's problems better if we make a rough separation of farms into several groups based on the volume or value of their production. In 1949, for example, there were 2,088,000 farms which produced a gross value of products of $2500 or more. This is less than half of the number—5,379,000 farms—enumerated by the census at that time. Yet these 2,088,000 farms which produced over $2500 in value of products per farm in 1949 accounted for 88 per cent of the value of all farm products marketed. They are the farms which produce for commercial markets; operated by farm families, these are called commercial family farms. There are, however, among the commercial farms 100,000 large-scale farms, most of which are not family farms; they produce about one-fourth of all farm products marketed.

The remaining 3,291,000 farms are a miscellaneous lot. All are small-scale units and many are part-time farms whose operators work off the farm a good part of the time. Census takers found that 1,030,000 of the farms were hardly more than rural residences, larger than 3 acres in size, but with farm sales averaging less than $250 in 1949.

Agricultural statisticians have analyzed the data to find out how many of these 3,291,000 farms are actually farms operated on a full-time basis by able-bodied families in their productive years. They found that fully half of the group were occupied by families deprived of the husband or wife, or the operator was under 25 or over 65 years of age, or operators or members of the family worked off the farm enough to bring the family income up to $2000 or more. The remaining 1,600,000 farms with less than $2500 of farm sales support the farm families that most people refer to when they speak of our low-income problem in agriculture.[1] These 1,600,000 low-income farms are almost as numerous as the commercial farms.

In 1953 the Department of Agriculture published an Agricultural Information Bulletin (No. 108) called *Low Production Farms*. This is one of the few available detailed studies of these farms. Low-production or low-income farms made up half or more of all farms in almost one-third of the counties in the United States. In 10 per cent of our counties, located mostly in the Appalachian areas and in

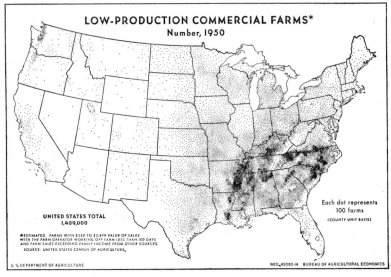

Figure 2

the South, low-production farms were 75 per cent or more of all farms.

While the heavy concentrations of low-production farms are found in the Appalachian Mountains, in the Mississippi Delta, and in the Southeast where cotton and tobacco are grown by sharecroppers, a substantial number of low-production farms are found in every state in the Union (Figure 2).

Farm leaders are and should be concerned with the low-income problem in agriculture for two basic reasons. First, children reared in

[1] *Technical Studies by the United States Department of Agriculture relating to select farm price support proposals*, House Committee on Agriculture, 83rd Congress, 2nd Session (Washington, D. C.: Gov't. Printing Office, 1954), p. 160.

the families in these low-income areas suffer from inferior education, often have inadequate diets, and do not have equality of opportunity as compared with the children of other rural families. Second, the workers in these families are only one-fourth to one-half as productive as those on the average commercial family farms. A number of studies in this field have been called studies of underemployment in agriculture. Obviously, the solution to the low-income problem in agriculture, in an over-all sense, is to increase the employment opportunities and the productivity of these workers.

Before going into the many proposed remedies for the low-income problem, however, we should explore more fully how these low-income areas "got that way."

Referring to Figure 2 again, we note that the heavy concentrations of low-production farms are found in the mountainous areas where the land is too rough for extensive farming and in the Southern states where cotton and tobacco are the leading crops.

Arthur Moore, in trying to find an explanation for low incomes or poverty in agriculture, points out in a National Planning Association pamphlet (No. 77) that "poor land" will not hold up as *the* explanation. He cites the high income and living standards on poor land in the Western ranching areas. He also dismisses the lack of ability on the part of the people on other poor land as *the* explanation. Studies show that these people do as well as the town-reared boys and girls when they move into urban areas and take industrial jobs.

We may get a better understanding of causal factors by looking at two different areas. The largest and most concentrated low-income area is the hilly area of Mississippi, Georgia, and west Tennessee where, in 1949, four-fifths of all the farms were full-time farms with less than $2500 total sales. Cotton is the major source of income. Most of the farmers own their land. Small fields, small farms, and hilly land are the prevailing pattern. Until recently, there has been little industrial development. The land and climate have permitted cotton growing and the production of subsistence crops sufficient to maintain a family. Up to the present, however, farmers in this area have not developed an extensive type of farming which would increase output per worker and increase family incomes up to the levels prevailing in the better farming areas. Many families and young people have left their communities to take nonfarm jobs in other parts of the country. Yet the uncertainty of jobs elsewhere and the cost of traveling a considerable distance to them have kept the remaining families from making a shift to higher-paying nonfarm jobs.

Let us look at two typical families, one in a hill-farm, the other in a mountain area.

The Jones Family

Sam and Sally Jones and their three children—Martha, age 13, Jimmie, 11, and Charles, 9—who live on a 50-acre farm in north-central Georgia know what it means to work hard yet have little to show for their effort. Both Sam and Sally were reared in the neighborhood and they now own free of debt the farm which had been farmed by Sam's parents for twenty-five years.

When they have the time to make comparisons, they can point with some pride to the progress they have made as compared with their parents. They now have electricity in the house and have a five-year old, second-hand car. Although Sally finished only the seventh grade and Sam the fourth grade, their children are still in school and they have plans for them to go to the consolidated high school. However, they haven't been able to get running water in the house yet, and Sam continues to farm with two old mules although he would like to get a small tractor.

Last year they had an allotment of 5.5 acres of cotton. In addition to cotton they produced 6 acres of corn and a few acres of lespedeza hay and miscellaneous crops. Less than half of their 50 acres was in crops. A milk cow, a growing heifer, a calf, three pigs for fall butchering, and a flock of twenty-five hens completed their farm picture.

When the Joneses totaled up their farm sales for 1954 they found they had sold $1000 worth of crops, mostly cotton, although they did sell some corn and oats. The cow was sold during the year, since the heifer would freshen next spring; and a little income from cream, poultry, and eggs brought total farm sales up to $1250.

Although the Joneses are busy all the daylight hours during the spring planting and fall harvest seasons, they are not burdened by farm work at other seasons. They have thought of improving their pastures and adding another cow but have never had the money necessary for fertilizer and seed and just haven't "gotten around to it."

Sam and Sally and their children produce most of their own food, including wheat which they exchange at the local mill for flour, and their living expenses are kept low by most standards. Sam finds that his cash farm expenses for seed, fertilizer, custom harvesting, feed supplements, and similar items amount to well over half of his farm sales. It is a good year when the Joneses have $700 to $800 available to spend on the family.

THE SMITH FAMILY

Another large area of low-production farms and low-income families includes the Blue Ridge Mountains of Virginia and North Carolina, and the Cumberland Mountains and Plateaus of West Virginia, Kentucky, and Tennessee. Parts of this area are highly industrialized, yet only a third of the farm operators spent a hundred or more days at nonfarm work in 1949. Agriculture is the leading industry, tobacco being the leading cash crop in parts of the area. Most of the farms produce a considerable quantity of products for home consumption. Because of the rugged country both fields and farms are small. Modern mechanized farming has not been adapted to these small rough farms.

The Smith family might be duplicated in any one of hundreds of valleys in the Appalachian Mountains. Tom and Mary Smith were married when Tom was 22 and Mary 19. For the first year they lived with Tom's parents and helped with the family farming operations.

Now in their late thirties they have a home and farm of their own, since Tom's father died early. They have five children ranging in age from 8 to 16 years and live in a three-room unpainted house of rough, sawed native lumber. As in most other houses along the branch, the main room is the kitchen where the meals are cooked and eaten and much of the work and "sitting" is done. The other two rooms are bedrooms. Two double beds in one room accommodate Tom and Mary and the two girls. The three boys share the other room.

All but the youngest of the Smith children help with the farm work in season. John, the oldest boy, quit school without finishing the eighth grade and sometimes, when farm work is slack, works in the woods for wages.

The Smith farm of 85 acres is an irregular piece of land extending for some distance on both sides of the branch. The 3 acres of bottom land are used for a large garden, a small corn and a small sorghum patch, and a hog lot.

Also, 5 or 6 acres of corn are grown on the 22 acres of open land on the lower slopes of the hillsides. The balance of this open land is used for hay and pasture. In most years one or more "patches" are idle because of a failure of seedings or a shortage of cash to purchase the necessary legume seeds. There are 60 acres of timber land higher up on the mountain slopes. Last year the Smiths didn't get anything off this woodland except a few fence posts for their own use and some firewood. Next year, however, they hope to cut for sale some fence posts and some poles for mine props.

Tom Smith keeps all the livestock his land will support—two dairy cows, two growing heifers, thirty chickens, one horse, and four pigs for home butchering. The wages earned by John, the oldest son, and Tom, working in the woods during the fall and winter months, were larger than the cash sales of eggs, cream, and veal calves.

When asked why they stayed on this farm in view of the job opportunities elsewhere, both Tom and Mary said they had sometimes talked of moving out of the mountains but somehow an opportunity had never presented itself. Anyway, Tom didn't think he would like regular indoor work day after day in a factory. He had worked at such a job for three months before marriage. When he was laid off he returned home. Then before going North to look for a job again he and Mary decided to get married. Tom's father became ill, they had children of their own, and one thing and another kept them from leaving home. Here they at least had food, beds, and shelter for their five children. John, the 16-year old son, had talked of going North to look for work but was uncertain where to look for a job.

Low-Income Areas a Result of Complex Forces

The stories of the Jones and the Smith families partly explain why we have such a concentration of low-income farms in one-third of our counties. Further light is thrown on the diverse factors responsible by reports from the states of New York and Kentucky.

In a Congressional study in 1951 the problem in the state of New York was described as follows:

There is no doubt that underemployment exists among open-country residents in some parts of New York State. Underemployment is most evident in agriculturally submarginal areas located beyond reasonable commuting distance to nonfarm employment. These areas are widely scattered. . . .

Many of the open-country unemployed are of the agriculturally disinherited—they and the land they are on have been technologically displaced. Land and people move slowly out of agriculture. A man seldom leaves farming once he has become established even though his income may be very low, unless, of course, he actually loses his farm by foreclosure. Most of the movement out of agriculture comes between generations. Even then it is slowed by the difficulty many young people meet in trying to get adequate training for reasonably remunerative nonfarm employment; slowed, also, by lack of information about nonfarm job opportunities and by a failure to understand the forces that have pushed and will continue to push rather large numbers of farms in this state below the margin at which they can support a reasonable level of living. There seems always the possibility that if the old farm were farmed as it should be it would be as good as any. They lack the grasp of the nature of the technological-limited-market squeeze that is slowly but very persistently shifting competitive advantages in favor of the farms that have the strongest physical resources.

The Congressional study described the problem in an area in eastern Kentucky in these words:

For two decades and more the economy of the quicksand area has failed to support itself. Many local people expect this situation not only to continue but to become even more pronounced. There are, indeed, numerous factors operating to this end. Population has a strong tendency to increase. The excessive periodic labor demands of the subsistence-farming units bind people to the area at the critical seasons. Workers are inclined to leave their families at home, where there is security and a sure, though small, livelihood, while they go out alone to work. These and the other powerful roots that the people have sunk into their home soil deter their migrating from the area more than temporarily.

Social scientists have not as yet developed fully satisfactory reasons to explain the many different pockets of low farm income or rural poverty in an otherwise enormously productive and wealthy industrial and rural economy. We know, for instance, that poverty breeds poverty. We know that lack of ready access to industrial jobs is a factor in many communities. Perhaps the most that can be said at the present time is that a whole complex of cultural, economic, and social factors has been responsible for the continued existence of these low-income areas.

Differences between the low-income areas and the better farming areas are much greater today than one hundred years ago when farming was largely a hand- and horse-power industry. In a sense the low-income problem in agriculture is the problem of living in the last half of the twentieth century with an eighteenth- and nineteenth-century type of agriculture and rural community.

Two Major Lines of Activity Needed

As we proceed to examine the solutions for the low-income problem in agriculture we should distinguish between families who are welfare cases and those who can solve their own problems under favorable conditions. Every community, whether rural or urban, has its families which are welfare cases because of sickness, permanent injury, or death of the breadwinner in the family. Then there are the unfortunate families in which husband and wife are separated and the remaining partner is unable to support the family. Finally, there may be a few families where the breadwinner, even in normal health, has not the ability to provide for a family. These families would be welfare cases in any community and are not considered a part of the low-income farm problem. Similarly, rural low-income families in which the head has reached retirement age are a part of the general welfare problem. When we refer to solutions for the low-income problem in agriculture we are concerned with solutions that will help the able-bodied family increase its productiveness two- or threefold and permit it to enjoy a level of living comparable to that obtaining in the better rural areas of the United States.

To most social scientists the solutions appear to be along two major lines, and progress is needed along both lines at the same time. On the one hand, a reduction is needed in the number of families depending on farming as a source of employment in these low-income rural areas. On the other hand, the economic opportunities of those who remain in agriculture must be increased by improved technology, increased credit resources, and in many cases by larger farming units.

Low-income farm families interested in finding nonfarm jobs could be assisted in a number of ways. The first step would be to determine the job opportunities available in different industries and different areas and make this information available in the low-income communities. We now have an elaborate research organization and informational setup to acquaint farmers with the economic outlook for dairying, cotton production, hogs, or any other crop or class of livestock. We have also a United States Employment Office with cooperative state and local offices. Yet we have not applied ourselves to this problem of evaluating prospective job opportunities with anything like the thoroughness with which we study the outlook for profits in hog-raising, dairying, and crop farming.

Along with a better informational service on job opportunities, we may need to give prospective migrants help in finding housing, in arranging financing to cover the period of transfer, and in making adjustments in a strange community. Assistance in establishing contact with persons from their home communities would ease the migrants' adjustments greatly. Surely public services of this character would promote general welfare as much as most educational and credit services now furnished farm families.

Another line of attack on this problem of encouraging more farm people to find employment outside of agriculture is to bring additional employment opportunities to these areas. Farm leaders working with local Chambers of Commerce and community service clubs may be helpful in getting new industries to locate in an area. Continued study of the economic possibilities of industrial development in low-income rural areas is one of the "solutions" advanced by all social scientists who have written about the problem.

Turning from consideration of solutions which lessen the communities' reliance on employment in agriculture to those which increase the families' productiveness in farming, we might start with a description of this problem as found in the earlier-mentioned community in eastern Kentucky:

Failure to use improved resources-management practices is a fundamental part of the subsistence organization. In farming, units are limited to small size by the existence of high peaks of labor demand, so that the family is able to produce only a small acreage of crops and a few livestock, principally for home needs. Labor peaks are heightened by the necessity for using poor land and by the high-labor intensity of the practices followed: nor is it usually economical to hire additional labor, even at low wage rates that prevail locally, to lighten the family's work burden at the peaks, so poor is the quality of the additional land that would be brought into use under such a system. Furthermore, failure to hire labor, as well as initial failure to use improved farm-management practices, stems in large measure from the smallness of the family's cash income, which tends to perpetuate practices requiring a minimum cash outlay.

Crop yields are lower and milk production per cow and egg production per hen are lower on these small low-income farms than on the larger commercial farms. The small, low-income farms use large amounts of labor to grow the same crops as are produced with power machinery on the larger farms. The reasons for the failure to develop more intensive farming systems on these small farms are many. The low-income farms often have poorer land than the commercial farms. As pointed out in the studies quoted earlier, these families usually are hard pressed for money to spend for seeds, fertilizers, modern machinery, foundation livestock, and supplies for disease and insect control. The farm operators in these families typically have attended school for only a few years. Many have been raised on diets deficient in some of the important nutritive elements, and the family has had inadequate medical and health services.

In spite of these handicaps, most social scientists are agreed that, except in the extremely rugged mountain areas, low-income farm families can double or triple their output on existing farms. They suggest that, even for families who must eventually obtain a larger farming unit to achieve a desirable level of efficiency, the first step should be the improvement of farming practices on the home farm.

The common statement that these low-income farm families have equal opportunity to benefit from educational, technical-assistance, and credit programs formulated for the benefit of all farm families overlooks important facts. To be of equal assistance to this group of farm families, programs must (1) put more emphasis on items which stimulate these people to acquire an interest in improving their practices; (2) adapt their educational materials to reach people with little formal education; and (3) integrate educational and credit programs in a manner that assures the availability of credit needed for the adoption of improved practices.

Where, because of hills, gullies, stones, or woods, small fields cannot be combined into an efficient operating unit for modern machinery, there is little hope of achieving average levels of productivity and income. Such communities will find their activities most rewarding if directed toward enlarging nonfarm employment opportunities. But, though many of the small-scale, low-income farms cannot be enlarged on an economic basis, farm enlargement is a "must" where conditions permit.

Where fields and farms can be combined, commercial farming can be achieved. Here again a coordinated effort is required. It involves (1) creating an awareness on the part of these families of the opportunities of higher levels of production and family living; (2) providing technical assistance in the adoption of improved farm and home practices; (3) making credit available both for land purchase and for increased working capital; and (4) encouraging and assisting families who would like to leave farming to find employment opportunities elsewhere, thereby permitting land holdings to become available for farm enlargement purposes.

REASONS FOR LACK OF PROGRESS

A brief review of these solutions for the low-income problem in agriculture put forward by the social scientists indicates how sharply it differs from many of the other agricultural problems. Solving the low-income problem in agriculture will be of little direct benefit to the families on commercial farms. Informed farm leaders from communities of average or above-average farms often have turned their backs on this problem, because it did not affect the welfare of their own communities and because they were busy with their own problems.

Local leaders within the low-income communities have not been effective in the past. All too often they are so poorly informed that they confuse rather than clarify the issues. Those who are well informed and are capable of playing a leadership role often have a special interest in maintaining the more than ample supply of labor in the community.

The major lines of solution proposed by the social scientists have been known for at least twelve or fifteen years and a number of the proposals for action were made even earlier. Current and past farm programs, while equally available to farms of all sizes, have not prevented a substantial widening of the gap between the low-income, underemployed farm families on small farms and the operators of commercial family farms. Some contend that the price-support programs actually have helped only the commercial farmers, leaving to the Farmers Home Administration the job of assisting low-income farmers.

Underlying the lack of progress on the low-income problem are mainly two sets of conditions. First, this sector of agriculture is poorly organized and has few spokesmen in group meetings and legislative halls. Second, the assumption that our public school and private enterprise systems give all people, including all rural families, equal opportunities for success has been widely held. Few subscribe fully to this assumption today, yet all too many farm leaders have taken the position that low income or poverty in agriculture is merely evidence of the family's lack of industry and ability. One way of putting it is that the Joneses and the Smiths have no one but themselves to blame if they continue to work small run-down farms and get little reward for their efforts.

The evidence presented earlier should do much to dispel this mistaken notion. The geographic concentration of these families in areas and regions suggests that it is in large part an environmental problem. Because of their physical and economic environment, these families are unable to make normal economic progress in our dynamic society. However, after accepting this view we are but little nearer socially acceptable solutions to the problem. Should we depend entirely on an improved school system and an enlightened private enterprise to improve gradually the opportunities for these poverty sectors of agriculture? Or should we take more direct remedial action along the lines suggested by the social scientists?

THE DILEMMA FOR FARM LEADERS

Farm leaders have an unusual challenge in this low-income problem. How much time and energy should farm leaders from the predominantly commercial farming areas devote to such problems? Since these low-income farm families are in a minority in farm organizations and in most rural organized groups, other views and problems—those of the majority—get priority in the public meetings. The successful farm leader must carry out the wishes of this majority. As a result, he tends to become fully occupied with the problems of the commercial sector of agriculture.

The problem is made more difficult by the fact that solutions of problems peculiar to the low-income families usually require some financial assistance from the rest of society. The proposals of the social scientists involve the use of public funds for such special educational, technical-assistance, and credit programs as will benefit primarily these low-income families. By what appeal can a farm leader mobilize support for activities which result in increased costs to members of his group?

For still another reason farm leadership has been slow to take action along the lines recommended by social scientists. While well over half of the 1,600,000 full-time farm families in the low-income group are farm owners, in many communities a substantial number are tenants and sharecroppers. An ample supply of tenants and sharecroppers in the community assures landowners that they can get their land farmed the way they wish on relatively favorable terms. Even the families of the owners of small farms are looked to by the owners of larger farms as a source of extra seasonal labor.

Programs and policies which encourage these tenant and sharecropper families to find nonfarm jobs will make it more difficult to find good tenants and sharecroppers, thus increasing the landowners' problems. Already higher wage rates in industry and the better opportunities elsewhere have made tenants, sharecroppers, and hired farm labor relatively (but not actually) scarce and high-priced in these low-production areas. Landowners are being forced to mechanize and change their systems of farming because of their inability to get tenants, sharecroppers, and hired labor as formerly. From their point of view the community is already suffering from unfair competition from industry. In the opinion of the larger farmers who have not changed their traditional systems of farming, there is little social, economic, or ethical basis for private and public programs that would decrease still further the local supply of tenants, sharecroppers, and hired labor in these low-income rural communities.

These are the major elements of the current farm-leadership dilemma regarding the low-income problem in agriculture.

On the one hand there is the evidence that the majority of the farm families in fairly large geographic areas have very low living standards and are only one-third to one-half as productive as the average farm or nonfarm family. Most of the benefits of current farm programs, including educational programs, are going to the families on commercial farms—permitting the situation of the low-income group to continue or even become worse. Communities made up largely of low-income families cannot support schools, or health, medical, and recreational programs comparable to those provided in the better rural areas.

On the other hand, current economic forces are giving rise to sufficient migration from these farms and communities to cause a shortage of local labor for the old cash-crop unmechanized systems of farming. Hired labor is high-priced relative to its productivity in traditional systems of farming.

The public currently supports state and national educational and informational programs for farmers. It also supports state and national programs of technical assistance and economic aid for farmers. To what extent should farm leaders, drawn largely from the commercial farms, assume responsibility for modifying these programs in ways that will result in increased benefits to low-income farm families?

Most informed farm leaders want to increase the proportion of the resources of public educational and assistance programs going to low-income rural areas. They reason that the entire country would be better off if the productivity and living standards of these families could be increased substantially. There is no formula, however, to guide them in deciding how much emphasis to place on these low-income problems. If increased emphasis on low-income problems can be achieved only at the expense of a reduction in programs for the families on commercial farms, the decision is particularly difficult.

The question how much increased emphasis should be given to educational, credit, and assistance programs for low-income farm families may well become one of the most important questions for farm leaders in the years ahead. President Eisenhower, in a special message to Congress in April 1955, recommended the adoption of a series of pilot programs for low-income farm families in fifty counties. In general, the programs recommended were those described in the preceding pages: special educational and credit facilities, improved labor placement services, and vocational training programs.[2]

It is expected that after some experience in these fifty pilot counties the successful programs will be extended to additional low-income areas. But the continued attack on the problem will depend as much on continued support from farm leaders outside low-income areas as on the demonstrated success of these pilot programs.

[2] The President's message incorporated many of the recommendations which had been developed by the United States Department of Agriculture: *Development of Agriculture's Human Resources—A Report on Problems of Low-income Farmers*, prepared for the Secretary of Agriculture, April 1955.

7

Are Hired Farm Workers a Disadvantaged Group?

Another problem that has had less attention from farm leaders than it deserves is the improvement of the social and economic conditions of hired farm workers. One reason for the lack of concern over such problems is that relatively few farm wage workers make hired work on farms a lifetime occupation. Most hired farm workers soon either become farm operators themselves or migrate to higher paid nonfarm jobs.

Many of the older hired farm workers have returned to farm work after spending a number of years in industrial jobs but find that they cannot continue indoor work for health reasons. Unlike substantial numbers in many other countries or the industrial workers in our own urban areas, few hired farm workers plan to spend the productive years of their life as farm wage workers. The few who do spend their entire lives as hired farm workers each year expect to be able to rent a farm of their own or transfer to a better paying nonfarm job in the near future. This rapid turnover of farm wage workers prevents the development of group solidarity and group spokesmen or leaders for hired farm workers comparable to the industrial labor leaders.

In recent years information regarding hired farm workers has substantially increased. In 1952 a special survey indicated that approximately 2 million people worked for wages on United States farms twenty-five days or more. But only 900,000 reported farm wage work as their chief activity throughout the year. Such uncertain statistics as are available for earlier years indicate that we may have reduced our hired farm workers by as much as 50 per cent in the last twenty-five years. Farm mechanization and high wages paid by urban employers have resulted in a sharp downtrend in both family and hired farm workers, but the decrease in wage workers has been more rapid. As a result a smaller share of the farm work is being done by hired farm workers today than in any recent period except perhaps during the war years.

THREE TYPES OF WORKERS

Hired farm workers may be classified in a number of ways. The statistical surveys in 1951 and 1952 indicate that about 20 per cent are female and 80 per cent are male workers. They also indicate that about one-third of the entire group are nonwhite, mostly Negroes, while two-thirds are white.

For our purposes, however, the most useful classification is: regular hired farm workers, migratory workers, and casual nonmigratory workers. Although the numbers in each of these groups change from year to year it is fairly accurate to say that in the early 1950s regular hired workers, those who work continuously on one farm most of the year, made up about one-third of all hired farm workers. Migratory workers, those who left their homes to work on farms outside their own communities, made up 20 to 25 per cent of the total. The remainder was made up of residents of the community who worked intermittently on different farms, worked part time at nonfarm wage work, or were partly self-employed. Only the first two of these groups, the regular hired workers and the migratory workers, are of direct concern to us in our study of social responsibility of farm leadership. The large group of nonmigratory casual farm wage workers are normally residents of their communities, differing from nonfarm workers only in that they spend a part of their time at farm wage work.

REGULAR HIRED FARM WORKERS

The one-third of the hired farm working force who work continuously on one farm for most of the year are often called regular hired workers. In 1953, 63 per cent of this group were married and 76 per cent were over 25 years of age. They earned an average of about $1200 in cash wages plus house rental and farm produce for the married families and board and room for the unmarried workers.

Twenty-nine per cent of the group earned $1500 or more. A higher proportion of these regular hired workers were white (80 per cent) than was true for all hired farm workers.

SOCIAL AND ECONOMIC PROBLEMS OF REGULAR HIRED FARM WORKERS

Regular hired farm workers' problems are primarily economic in character. Hired farm workers' families generally are accepted in the rural communities without discrimination. Children from workers' families attend the same schools and churches as the children from the employers' families. Low wages, poor housing, and the absence of the benefits of industrial workers' legislation are the chief complaints of hired farm workers today. These three problems will be examined separately to determine the extent to which further progress can be expected as the result of the activities of farm leaders.

All statistical data of farm and nonfarm wage rates indicate that the wages paid farm workers, including house rental and produce, are lower than the average wages paid industrial workers. Each year there are approximately twice as many farm boys reaching working age as there are farms vacated by the retirement or death of the farm operator. Some of these boys may find wage employment on farms. Others will go directly to nonfarm jobs. But rural communities always have a potential excess supply of local labor. This tends to keep farm wage rates at the bottom of the wage scale.

A second important factor is the low value of farm production per worker. Farm operators find that they cannot afford to pay hired workers the equivalent of industrial wages and at the same time earn a fair return for their own labor and investment.

Farm leaders complain about the high wages paid by industry and give far too little thought to ways and means of improving the efficiency of farming operations so that they can afford to pay higher wages. Without attempting to establish a minimum wage level for hired farm workers, it is apparent that when their yearly cash wages averaged only $1200 in 1951, even though they received free house rental and some farm-raised produce, a substantial proportion of them must have had great difficulty in supporting a family. Surely the responsibility of farm leaders in the general farm organizations includes a concern for the welfare of these hired farm workers' families with inadequate incomes.

In most cases the problem is not exploitation of the worker by his employer; rather it is the problem of the low level of farm earnings and the below-average earnings of some farmers who have not yet adopted modern machinery and improved husbandry practices. In many cases the farm employer who cannot afford to pay more than the lowest wage scales is himself partially responsible in that he has not modernized his farming methods and increased his farming operations so as to fully utilize labor-saving machinery available.

Farm leadership can assist hired farm workers indirectly by working toward an improvement in farming efficiency and an improvement in farm earnings through more adequate market-improvement and price-stabilization programs. To a large extent the same types of remedies proposed by the social scientists for the low-income problem would be helpful in improving the competitive position of the lower-paid hired farm workers. While there are no adequate studies of hired farm workers' housing available, it is believed that the housing of the lower-paid hired farm workers is as inadequate as their wage level. Some of the poorest rural housing for both hired workers and operators' families is found on owner-operated farms in the South, in the mountain valleys, and in other low-income communities.

On the other hand, on many of the northern livestock farms one finds comfortable, modern, and attractive housing for the hired worker's family. In an effort to meet the competition of nonfarm employers, many farmers have improved and modernized their hired men's houses in recent years. Difficulty in getting and keeping a good hired worker has been the greatest incentive to the improvement of hired workers' housing in the past. It is doubtful that any other incentive will prove to be as effective as this competitive influence.

Farm families are motivated by many other factors, however, in addition to the economic motive. The level of housing in a rural community depends in part, but only in part, on the level of incomes in that community. One of the responsibilities of farm leaders is to inspire and assist farm families to achieve higher standards in those aspects of living which can be accomplished through their own personal efforts. Improved housing for both the farm operators and the hired farm workers' families in the less productive sections of the United States falls into this category. During slack seasons in the farming operations much could be done with local materials and at relatively little expense to improve housing conditions.

INCREASED SECURITY AND PROTECTION FOR HIRED FARM WORKERS

Individual states vary in the extent to which the benefits of legislation for the security and protection of industrial workers are made available to regular hired farm workers. For the most part, however, hired workers on family farms where only one or two workers are employed are not protected by workmen's compensation insurance or its equivalent while at work. A large proportion of the industrial workers now have group hospitalization and life insurance, partially financed by the employers. Relatively few hired farm workers have such protection.

While regular hired farm workers are now included in the Social Security coverage and hence may become eligible for retirement pensions, they are not yet eligible for unemployment compensation. By almost any comparisons hired farm workers' families have less protection against accidents, sickness, and unemployment than their urban relatives. There are offsetting factors, however. The employer may voluntarily carry insurance for his employee and in any case is likely to be more generous than an urban corporation in assisting his family in case of accident or sickness.

SUMMARY

We return now by way of a summary to the key question raised by this chapter. Are hired farm workers a disadvantaged group and what is the social responsibility of farm leadership in this area? (It should be noted that the problems of migratory workers have been left for the next chapter.)

There are wide differences in the incomes, living conditions, and the protection and security of regular hired farm workers. Many of these hired farm workers have better incomes and living conditions than the owner and tenant families on the low-income farms. As compared with the owner families on commercial farms and the workers on industrial jobs, however, hired farm workers appear to be at a disadvantage.

Low wage levels and living conditions of the lower-paid hired farm workers are usually not the result of deliberate exploitation by the employer. He may be having just as difficult a problem as the hired farm worker because of low prices for his products, because of his out-of-date management practices, or because he is trying to make a living on an inadequate farm.

Improvement for the regular hired farm workers appears to lie in three directions: (1) improved efficiency of farm employers and more adequate market-improvement and price-stabilization programs which will permit the payment of higher wages, (2) higher standards in those aspects of living which can be achieved without much cash expenditure, and (3) improvement of the general labor market so that the lower-paid hired farm workers having the most unsatisfactory living conditions will have opportunities to shift to better paying jobs.

8

Migratory Workers: A Special Problem

Problems of migratory workers have often been news in recent years. The plight of these workers has been vividly depicted as the plight of a group who move restlessly over the face of the land, but do not belong to the land; nor does the land belong to them. They work in community after community, but they neither claim the community as home nor does the community claim them. Domestic migrants are citizens of the United States but they are scarcely more a part of the land of their birth than the alien migrants who may be working beside them.[1]

The Department of Agriculture estimates that there were in 1952 about 450,000 of these domestic migratory workers including the children under 14 years of age who worked in the fields. In addition a large number of Mexican nationals came into the country, both legally and illegally, for temporary farm work, as they have been doing every year, especially since World War II.

Roughly two-thirds of these migratory workers were male and one-third female. Those under 14 years of age were not counted officially. Of those 14 years of age or older, 40 per cent were under 25 years of age, 43 per cent were 25 to 44, and 17 per cent were 45 or older. These people worked for an average of 168 days, mostly on farms, and received $902 in cash wages for their entire year's work. Only one-third of these migratory workers were employed as many as 250 days at both farm and nonfarm work, while one-third worked fewer than 75 days.

IMPORTANCE OF MIGRATORY WORKERS

Migratory workers are employed on farms fewer days a year than nonmigratory workers. For this reason they do not contribute to farm

[1] *Migratory Labor in American Agriculture,* Report of President's Commission on Migratory Labor (1951), p. 3.

output in proportion to their numbers. They supply 3 to 4 per cent of the total labor used to produce the nation's farm output.

Migratory labor is employed principally in cotton, fruits, vegetables, and sugar beets. A small proportion of these migratory workers are employed for short seasons on family farms which grow some sugar beets, truck crops, or fruits. The principal employers of migratory labor are the large industrial farms which made up 2 per cent of all commercial farms but which accounted for 26 per cent of the value of all products sold in 1949. This group of farms accounted for 42 per cent of all expenditures for hired farm labor, both migratory and nonmigratory, in that year.

NATURE OF MIGRATORY WORKER PROBLEM

The migratory labor problem is confined to relatively few worker families, a small percentage of the farms, and relatively few communities. Yet the problems associated with migratory labor are some of our most pressing social and economic problems in those communities which require the services of migratory labor to produce and harvest their crops. In the fruit and truck crop sections where migrant laborers are employed, as the crops mature farmers anxiously await their coming; then, as the harvest closes, the community with equal anxiety awaits their going.

The dilemma faced by farm employers requiring large numbers of seasonal laborers is that they want a labor supply ready and willing to work when needed, but do not want to incur social and economic obligations on themselves and their communities when the seasonal work is finished. The employer often attempts to meet these conditions by dealing with a crew leader who agrees to have the required number of workers on the job when wanted and to transport them to other communities when the job is finished.

The migrant worker thus finds he must deal with a crew leader if he wishes seasonal work. His employment is undependable because of the uncertainty of the weather and the tendency of employers to overstate their labor requirements for particular jobs. If labor is available, it is to the employer's advantage to have a large crew harvest his crop in a few days when it is at its prime, rather than to have a smaller crew at work for a longer period. In periods of slack labor demand there is often over-recruitment and enforced idleness for many workers; they are idle also when jobs are finished ahead of time before other employers are ready for them. On the other hand, employers have large investments in their crops and must be assured of an ample supply of labor to tend and harvest them. If necessary, arrangements must be made to bring in workers from long distances, as from Mexico, Puerto Rico, and Jamaica.

While many of both the domestic and the alien migrant workers are single individuals who have left their families at home, the majority of such workers are family groups who travel and work together as a family unit working at piece-rate wages and pooling their earnings. This gives rise to what is probably the most serious social problem associated with migratory labor, a failure to give the children of the migrant families a fair start in life. Although there has been great progress in recent years, children in migrant families often continue to suffer from inadequate sanitary and health standards in their daily living and are unable to obtain an adequate public school education.

The Tucker Family

A brief description of the Tucker family will indicate the problems encountered by migrant worker families. John and Sarah Tucker, 44 and 36 years of age respectively, have six daughters and three sons varying in age from 20 years down to 2. The oldest is a son; and two other sons are 5 and 2 years old respectively. Several years ago the Tuckers left their home in Mississippi and came to the Everglades area of Florida to obtain seasonal work in vegetable production. The entire family work whenever they have an opportunity, although only John and his oldest son have anything like steady work. For several years they have been going for four to five months each year to Maryland, where the two men work in a cannery.

The Tuckers report that on working days they catch a truck about 6 or 6:30 A.M. and may ride fifty or sixty miles on the crowded truck to the field. If the work is bean picking they may have to wait two hours for the dew to dry off the beans. If there is plenty of work for the entire crew, they will work until 6 P.M. and then ride home in the truck, getting home between 8 and 10. If the work is completed earlier in the day, they get paid for the number of bushels of beans picked, and the day's time and effort may return only part of a day's pay.

Since moving from Mississippi the Tuckers have not tried to settle down. When interviewed they were living in a housing project in two rooms of a four-room, metal, barrack-type building constructed by the government for migrant workers. Other families in the housing project had come from Alabama, Mississippi, Georgia, and the Carolinas.

The oil cookstove in one of the rooms is used to heat it on cold days as well as to prepare the meals. When it is warm and the sun shines, the metal walls overheat the rooms; when it is cold and cloudy the rooms are cold. The two rooms are not connecting, and the Tuckers must go outside to get from one room to the other. Each room has one ceiling outlet for electricity. The window openings are screened, but metal doors rather than glass windows are used to close them in bad weather. When visited, the Tuckers were paying $5.50 weekly for these two rooms furnished with the three-burner oil stove, a kitchen table, two chairs, and two beds.

When they go to Maryland they have rent-free housing in connection with their cannery work. The two men each worked a total of 35 weeks and the Tucker family earnings in 1949 amounted to $1900. Both John and Sarah Tucker had finished the tenth grade, but their oldest son Edward dropped out of school when he finished the eighth grade in order to help support the family. It is doubtful that the older girls will complete as much school work as their parents had.[2]

The migrant families' problems stem from the way state and local regulations have been developed. These regulations are primarily to serve and protect the local residents. A family that cannot claim local residence finds most of the communities' public services and legal protections unavailable to it.

The migrant worker family is a special problem to virtually every public agency established to protect the public welfare. It is a special problem to the school officials, the public health authorities, the local welfare agency, the police, and the employment agency. The correction of abuse of the rights of migrant families in a particular

[2] Information on the Tucker family was taken from *Making Ends Meet on Less than $2,000 a Year,* Joint Committee on the Economic Report, 82nd Congress, 1st Session (Washington, D. C.: Gov't. Printing Office, 1951), pp. 58-59.

community, if it is assumed that they should have rights comparable to those of the local residents, frequently requires the participation of several of these agencies.

WHAT CAN BE DONE?

Without attempting to develop the social and economic problems of the migrants and the communities that utilize their labor services, let us turn to some of the suggested solutions. A group of responsible citizens[3] have proposed that employers should take responsibility for compliance with child labor and school attendance laws; adequate housing, either individually or jointly with neighbors; planning farming operations to reduce seasonal labor requirements; and cooperation with churches, schools, and other community organizations to assure that the community's health, school, and recreational facilities are available to the migrants.

Some state governments have already demonstrated their concern for the problems of migrants by establishing minimum standards for housing, providing health clinics, extending school attendance legislation to cover children of migratory workers, providing supervisory control over private labor contractors and expanding their farm recruitment and placement services. Legislation of this type is needed in all states utilizing migrant labor.

A large part of the solution to the migrant workers' problems must be found in the communities and states where the migrants are employed. The Federal government, however, may assist in a number of areas.

The President's Commission on Migratory Labor in 1951 recommended that all foreign labor importation and contracting be under the terms of intergovernmental agreements and that Federal legislation be adopted to prohibit interstate recruitment of farm labor by crew leaders, labor contractors, and others, except when such agents are licensed by the Department of Labor. They also urged the extension of Federal and state unemployment compensation, legislation to cover agricultural labor and increased grants of Federal funds to states on a matching basis for use in meeting the health, school, and welfare problems of communities where migrant workers are employed.

[3] National Planning Association Pamphlet No. 82 (Washington, D. C., 1953).

SOCIAL RESPONSIBILITY IN THE MIGRATORY LABOR FIELD

Someone has said there is no other major problem in American rural life about which so much has been said and written and so little action taken. The reasons for this are similar to those advanced for the lack of action on problems having to do with low-income farm families. The migrant families have few defenders in public meetings and legislative halls. The migrants themselves are a changing group, settling down and taking root in a community only when economic conditions permit.

Farm leaders are more or less familiar with the situation and problems outlined earlier in this chapter. In many communities they have taken action to improve housing, health, school attendance, and the working conditions of migrant worker families. Farm leaders outside the communities where migrant labor is employed have more than an altruistic interest, however, in the improvement of these conditions. Employers utilizing this "cheap" labor which lives under substandard conditions are in competition with farm families and employers attempting to maintain higher standards. In the interest of maintaining their own living standards farm leaders in communities having no migrant labor may be expected to show increasing concern regarding migrant workers' living standards and working conditions.

Migrant-worker families are in the weakest bargaining position in our entire society. They would not be migrants if they were satisfied with their family earnings in their home communities. Away from home, in a strange community without savings, they must accept the wages, working conditions, and housing offered them. Unless farm leaders with a sense of social responsibility support legal restraints which prevent individual employers from taking undue advantage of this weak bargaining position, not only will the communities and the future citizens coming from this sector of our population suffer, but the competition of these employers with lower labor costs will tend to lower living standards in their own rural communities. Farm leaders most familiar with this problem recognize that if the principle of fair play is applied in this area it would result in substantial improvements.

Perhaps the most we can expect of farm leaders is that they take time to become familiar with the migrants' problems in the various areas where they are employed and support such programs for dealing with them as conscience dictates. Some farmers have an economic motive for not improving the treatment of migrant workers. And farm groups are organized primarily to achieve the goals of their members, not the welfare of others with whom they do business. They are occupied with their own problems. Perhaps we must look mainly to others, such as local, state, and national church organizations, the National Council on Agricultural Life and Labor, The National Child Labor Committee, and similar groups to take the initiative in bringing about needed improvements in the treatment of migrant workers.

9

Achieving Land Tenure
and Credit Improvements

There is general agreement among most farm leaders that substantial improvements are needed in our land tenure arrangements. We are proud of the fact that United States agriculture is predominantly made up of family farm owners. In 1950, 72.7 per cent of the farms enumerated by the census were operated by owners. This is the highest proportion of farms operated by owners since 1880. It is an achievement to be proud of but it does not mean that our tenure problems have been solved.

Needed improvements in land tenure arrangements most often mentioned include leasing practices which give tenants more security and provide for compensation for unexhausted improvements—i.e. improvements the full benefit of which the tenant does not remain long enough to derive; reorientation of any and all government policies which now encourage corporate farming rather than family farm ownership and operation; improvement in the methods of transferring the family farm from one generation to the next; improvement of tenure and credit practices for young people starting in farming; and additional credit and farm planning assistance for families desiring to enlarge and develop existing inadequate farming units.

All too often a rented farm is a run-down farm. Not all rented farms are run-down, but there are enough such to cause many people to look on farm tenancy as a social evil. On many rented farms soil fertility is depleted, fences are allowed to deteriorate, and needed building repairs are neglected because the tenants have no assurance of staying long enough to benefit from better farming practices. The landlord who might prevent this from happening lives too far away or is too indifferent to require that better farming practices be followed. Or the landlord may be a widow who must use all available income from the farm for family living and debt service. When the income from a farm is divided between two families and a finance company there may not be much left for needed upkeep.

Several worthwhile approaches to the solution of this problem are available. One is an educational program directed toward both the landlord and the tenant. Long-term amortized financing of indebtedness is another improvement needed on many farms. Increased restrictions on the tenant's use of the land and written leases placing the responsibility for specific repairs definitely on either the tenant or the landlord would do much to prevent situations from arising where both the landlord and the tenant believe that the responsibility for the repairs rests on the other party. Finally, state legislation might be adopted that would give tenants more security of tenure and assure compensation for unexhausted improvements. This would encourage tenants to make many more repairs and improvements. All these alternatives merit attention.

The greatest possibilities of improvement in existing practices, however, are believed to be in giving tenants more assurance that they may stay on the farm long enough to benefit from good management practices and that they will be repaid for their investment if they should leave before the benefits are all realized. Iowa, for example, now has legislation requiring landlords and tenants to give notice several months before the end of the lease year if they expect to terminate the lease. If such notice is not given by either the landlord or the tenant, the existing leasing arrangements continue in effect for the following year. If either the tenant leaves or the landlord requires that the farm be vacated on short notice at the end of the year damages may be assessed against the party that failed to give adequate notice. Since it is the states, rather than the Federal government, which have the basic authority to legislate in the land tenure field, legislation along this line is needed in many additional states in the interest of better farming practices on rented farms.

A group of representatives of land grant colleges in 1944 made the following statement:

Every landlord and tenant should be urged to prepare a written lease that is fair to both parties. However, in order to protect the interest of both landlord and tenant, each state in which tenancy is important should establish in its statutes a basic lease which will govern in the absence of such written agreements. An essential feature of such a lease should provide a fair division of income from a system of farming that is profitable to both landlord and tenant.

To encourage good farming practices and to promote desirable tenure conditions, state laws are needed establishing minimum housing standards, providing compensation for disturbance without cause, protecting owners against misuse of their property, and providing reimbursement to the tenants for unexpended improvements made by them. Both parties should be required to give adequate notice of lease termination. Local arbitration committees can well be employed to handle grievances, adjust differences, and assist in determining equitable rental rates.

Because in many states the sharecropper has no specific legal right either as a tenant or farm laborer, legislation is badly needed to establish his status. Greater security and an improved status would result if such legislation gave tenant rights to all persons sharing a crop with the landlord.[1]

Slow Progress of Improvement in Tenure Relations

There are two major reasons for the slow progress in the improvement of tenure relations in the United States. First, we have tended to look on farm rental as a temporary stage in a family's progress toward farm ownership, and as a temporary situation for the farm while passing from one owner-operator to another. Family farm ownership is one of our more important rural goals, and we have been much more interested in promoting farm ownership than in improving the conditions under which farms are rented.

Second, except for the Southern Tenant Farmers Union, which became inactive after a few years, tenants have not organized to advance their group interests. Most farm leaders, by the time they have achieved a position of leadership, have become farm owners. The particular problems associated with farm tenancy seem unimportant as compared with farm price stabilization, marketing, disease control, and the many other problems which affect all farmers whether owners or tenants. Only in communities where a high proportion of the farms are operated by tenants each year is there much appreciation of the need for improvement in the legislation and practices governing farm rental.

[1] Association of Land Grant Colleges, *Post War Agricultural Policy* (October 25, 1944), p. 37.

As might be expected in a relatively new country where most farm families look forward to owning their own farms, the leasing practices and the written leases have tended to place major emphasis on the landlords' interests. This overemphasis on the landlords' interest and the underemphasis on the tenants' point of view has been corrected in lease forms prepared by the staff members of the land grant colleges and the United States Department of Agriculture in recent years.

It seems probable, however, that improvements in tenure relations will continue to make slow progress as long as a high proportion of our farms are owner-operated and tenants are a constantly changing, unorganized group. Farm leadership encounters many of the same problems and has much the same social responsibility in this area as in the improvement of opportunities for the low-income farm families.

Especially in the communities where a substantial part of the farms are rented, improvement in tenure relations would do much to improve the entire community. Both landlords and tenants would realize higher incomes and better living conditions over a period of years. Tenants would take a greater interest in community affairs. Soil resources would be conserved. Yet the farm leader finds other problems more pressing. This is an unfortunate situation. Farm leadership is not living up to its responsibilities in the tenure relations field.

Policies to Encourage Family Farm Ownership

Approximately 98 per cent of all farms are operated by farm families. The number of farms by economic class in 1950 is shown in Table I.

As already noted, agricultural policies throughout our entire national life have been influenced by a national concern to promote and maintain family farm ownership and operation. Passage of the preemption and homestead laws, establishment of the Land Grant Colleges, Agricultural Experiment Stations, and Extension Services, the tenant-purchase Bankhead-Jones Act of 1937, and the creation of the Federal Land Bank System are a few of the more important legislative developments resulting from this national desire for widespread family farm ownership in the United States.

Many individuals and groups are concerned at the present time

TABLE I. FARMS AND FARM SALES BY ECONOMIC CLASS,
UNITED STATES CENSUS OF 1950

Class	Value of Sales	Per Cent of all Farms	Per Cent of all Farm Sales
Commercial farms			
1. Large scale (many corporate owned)	$25,000 and over	2	26
2. Large (mostly family farms)	10,000—24,999	7	25
3. Medium (family farms)	5,000— 9,999	13	23
4. Small (family farms)	2,500— 4,999	16	14
5. Very small (family farms)	1,200— 2,499	17	7
6. Inadequate (family farms)*	250— 1,199	13	2
Other farms			
Part-time*	250— 1,199	12	2
Residential	——	20	1
Total farms: 5,379,000		100	100

* Operator worked off-farm less than 100 days and farm sales were greater than other income.

* Operator worked off-farm 100 days or more and other family income was greater than sales from the farm.

about the future of the family farm. They are afraid that the same technological and economic forces which have led to the creation of the large corporation in business are now leading to large-scale farming. Thus far there is little evidence to justify their fears. Although farm units are growing in size, studies by specialists in the United States Department of Agriculture indicate that farms have not increased in size in the last twenty years in as great a proportion as farm operation has increased in efficiency. As a result, the average farm today employs a smaller amount of family and hired farm labor than in any recent period.

In this connection it is encouraging to note that a thorough student of this problem concludes that mechanization is an incentive for larger than family farms only in the case of highly specialized farming.[2] This is not conclusive evidence of the continued vigor of the family farm. On the other hand, there is no evidence of rapid

[2] John M. Brewster, "The Machine Process in Agriculture and Industry," *Journal of Farm Economics*, Vol. XXXII, No. 1, p. 72.

growth in the number and importance of large-scale farms. Both in 1940 and 1950 the large-scale farms, making up 2 per cent of the number of all farms, accounted for about 25 per cent of all farm sales. Sometime in the future large-scale farms depending primarily on hired labor may be able to produce and market products more efficiently than family farms, but there is little evidence of a strong trend in that direction at the present time.

Large-scale farms at present are primarily specialty farms, often employing large numbers of migratory workers during the planting, cultivation, and harvest seasons. During the remainder of the year a small maintenance crew is all that is necessary at the farm. Thus far, large-scale livestock farms and ranches employing crews of farm workers are rare except in the intermountain regions. Apparently it is difficult to hire good livestock herdsmen and supervise them adequately when they are employed in substantial numbers. Also, the care of livestock cannot be fully reduced to a routine.

Even though there does not appear to be a decline in the relative importance of the family farm, it is appropriate to keep agricultural policies under constant review in order to evaluate their effect on the achievement and maintenance of family farming goals. Farm price-support programs in particular need continued study and modifications from time to time from this point of view. Continued support of cooperative credit and cooperative marketing and purchasing are largely justified as necessary, or at least very helpful, corollaries of family farming. Continued public support of research and extension makes technological progress fully as rapid on family farms as in typical large industrial corporation.

Many of the public policies of benefit to farmers tend to encourage expansion in farm size. They may be opposed for this reason even though on further analysis it develops that the policies merely encourage family farms to expand from small or medium size to larger family farming units.

Farm leaders have both a negative and a positive role in safeguarding family farming. They must guard against public policies that encourage a trend toward larger-scale units than family farming requires. At the same time, they need to sponsor policies and programs that will assist families on inadequate farming units to increase their scale of operations if they are to be fully effective in promoting the type of family farming which makes a contribution to our democracy.

IMPROVEMENTS IN TRANSFERRING FAMILY
FARMS WITHIN THE FAMILY

Only in recent years have social scientists and farm leaders given attention to the problem of transferring the family farm from one generation to the next. In earlier years when new land was waiting in the West and off-farm jobs were readily available, little thought was given to the problems families encounter when trying to arrange for a son to take over the farming operations. The parent-to-son farm transfer problem is widespread because most farms are too small to support two families.

A son or son-in-law is often ready to take over the operation of a farm at the age of 22 to 28 when the parents are 55 years of age or even younger. If the farm is large enough to utilize fully two workers, a father-son partnership can be undertaken on a basis satisfactory to both parties. The more typical situation, however, involves a farm family on a farm already too small by modern standards for one family. In spite of this the parents would like to have the young folks take over the farm eventually and so try to accommodate the newly-married son.

In such circumstances many stresses and tensions develop between the two families; even hardships may be endured in sharing an inadequate income and a one-family residence. Clearly, farm leaders should encourage families to make plans for an adequate operating unit if the son or son-in-law is to take over operation of the farm. In communities where additional land is not available to enlarge a small farming unit, either the young family or the older family will find it more satisfactory to take an off-farm job or the young family may rent a neighboring farm for a period.

In the interest of both productive efficiency and family happiness, the current practice of many farm families of sharing an inadequate farm with the married son and his family should be discouraged. The primary goal and ambition of many farm families, however, is to see one or more of their children established on the home farm carrying forward the family enterprise. These families are the backbone of our rural communities. We shall have better rural communities and more efficient farming when a higher proportion of our farm families establish such goals and are successful in building up an adequate farm unit and a father-son partnership for operating it. Probably no activity of farm leaders will be more satisfying over a period of years than developing community programs that have as their goal helping farm families build up adequate-size farms and improve their practices in transferring the farming business to the children.

IMPROVING CONDITIONS FOR THE BEGINNING FARMERS

Beginning farmers today, if they are to operate an efficient farming unit, require three to four times as much capital investment as fifteen years ago. Because of the current high capital investment required in farming, many people believe that beginning farmers have a more difficult time than in earlier years. The problem is most acute for the son of a hired worker or a tenant who has been unable to accumulate a good set of farming equipment and a herd of livestock.

In every farming community there are several capable young men who are beginning farming for themselves and who do not have successful parents to help them. The young man who inherits a half interest in a small run-down farm is little if any better off than the young man without prospect of inheritance.

The mechanical equipment and livestock on typical family-operated farms require an investment of $9000 to $14,000 in Northern states and $4000 to $6000 in the South (except Texas). Farmers now have five and a half times as much invested in machinery as in the prewar years. A minimum-size family farm, including land and non-real-estate capital, requires an investment of $20,000 to $40,000 in the Northern states.[3]

It is next to impossible for young families to save enough as laborers or tenants to cover the working capital needs of a modern farm in addition to supporting a growing family. The serious aspect of the "beginning farmer" problem is not that many who would like to start farming are prevented from starting (as pointed out earlier, there is no shortage of farmers); it is rather that even the competent young couples who manage to start are prevented from developing beyond a barely living existence.

[3] Robert K. Buck *Beginning Farmers, A Vulnerable Group in American Agriculture.* (Washington: August 1954), p. 5. Agriculture Committee Report, National Planning Association Pamphlet No. 88.

INTERMEDIATE CREDIT AND SPECIAL TRAINING NEEDED

From the beginning farmers' point of view, the present farm credit facilities are inadequate. They can get either short-term credit, up to twelve months, or long-time real estate credit if they have the necessary equity capital. But they cannot get credit for working capital with three- to seven-year repayment schedules.

Such surveys as have been made show that most loans to young farmers by commercial credit institutions are for one-year periods or less. In many cases the repayment of loans in such short periods prevents these young farmers from developing efficient farming programs. Special management-training programs also are needed for these young families.

An objective appraisal of the difficulties of beginning farmers at the present time as compared with earlier years must stress the importance of relative cost, price, and profit levels as compared with earlier periods. Until 1951 or 1952, at least, capital investment requirements had not increased any more rapidly than income-earning opportunities in farming. A young farmer who could borrow the money to stock and equip a rented farm of adequate size could repay his debts as easily as the beginning farmer twenty years earlier. On the other hand, if farming costs continue high in the future while farm prices slip further, beginning farmers may be unable to repay their loans even though the repayment period is several years.

Farm leaders have shown great interest in satisfactory cost-price relationships in agriculture—one of the primary requisites for beginning farmers. The increase in capital requirements in farming has increased the credit, risk, and management skills needed by beginning farmers, however, even though satisfactory cost-price relationships prevail. Farm leaders have shown too little interest in this aspect of beginning farmers' problems which, on the whole also, have had little organized attention from farm leaders in spite of the extent to which they have been discussed at informal farmers' meetings.

The remedies, insofar as remedies are available, appear to be improvement in farm loan practices, improvement in leasing practices, and increased attention to this younger group of farmers in the public educational programs.

INCREASED CREDIT AND TECHNICAL ASSISTANCE FOR FARM ENLARGEMENT AND DEVELOPMENT

A full discussion of this topic would duplicate parts of the discussion on the low-income farm problem. However, the need for additional credit and technical assistance for farmers with ability and ambition who find themselves on inadequate farms should be mentioned at this time to supplement the discussion of needed tenure and credit improvements.

An unpublished United States Department of Agriculture staff report on this topic stated that a concerted and organized effort should be made to encourage private and cooperative lenders to make more loans to enlarge, develop, stock, and equip presently inadequate farms. It stated also that consideration should be given to appropriate changes in the policy and regulations which would result in an increase of three- to ten-year amortized loans from both the commercial banking and cooperative credit systems.

With appropriate policies of encouragement and assistance, commercial and cooperative lending institutions should greatly increase their loans to present low-income farmers. There will remain, however, a substantial number of potentially efficient full-time farmers who cannot qualify for commercial credit even though present credit practices are modified. Such farmers turn to the Farmers Home Administration for assistance. The Farmers Home Administration should be able to accelerate its program of farm enlargement and development loans as a part of the program for low-income farmers recommended in the President's special message to Congress in April 1955.

In summary, leaders in general farm organizations have given much less attention to needed tenure and credit improvements in the last two decades than their importance merits. The tenure and credit practices in the rural communities underlie other problems such as soil conservation, school and church improvements, financial progress of young farm families, and the rate of adoption of improved farming methods. Farm leaders in the future will surely have to give these problems more of their attention.

10

Farm Leadership in Soil Conservation

In the field of soil conservation in the United States farm leaders have great opportunities and responsibilities. Although much progress has been made in the past twenty years, approximately half of our crop land continues to suffer from serious erosion losses. American farmers are still drawing down the great reserves of natural resources which were discovered in this country.

A recognition of this situation led the Council for Social Action of the Congregational Christian Churches to adopt in 1950 a policy declaration on conservation of natural resources which affirmed: "The Christian conception of human brotherhood requires that we conserve, develop, use, and share our natural wealth in ways that will contribute to advancement, justice, and peace throughout the world." This is not a new conception of Christian stewardship, yet in spite of the fact that we consider ourselves a Christian nation and farmers are one of the most religious groups in the country, soil and forestry resources have been used up at a rapid rate. Only a fraction of the original productive topsoil and of the original plant nutrients remain to be passed on to our children and grandchildren. A recent Government pamphlet included this compelling statement: "The Nation is still using its soil resources at a rate faster than it is building them up."[1]

Two Sets of Issues Involved

In reviewing this record—which is far from the Christian ideal— and in deciding on the nature of social responsibility of farm leaders in this field, two sets of issues move into the foreground. The first

[1] *Soil and Water Conservation Loans*, House Agricultural Committee, 83rd Congress, 2nd Session (Washington, D. C.: Gov't Printing Office, August 18, 1954), p. 1.

set is concerned with the extent to which we should conserve. The second is concerned with appropriate methods to use in achieving and maintaining the desired level of conservation.

To What Extent Should We Conserve?

There can be no argument regarding the present state of conservation activities. They are inadequate. Yet in our present hindsight we cannot justly blame our ancestors for lack of foresight in their land-clearing activities and their eagerness for immediate use of resources. Indeed it might well be argued that we are far better off to have drained down some of the accumulated store of fertility in the topsoil, when it seemed almost inexhaustible and to have built up our investment in schools, churches, roads, and the education of our children. Many of our fine rural community developments today are the result of the transfer of original soil fertility assets into assets in the form of schools, roads, libraries, and well-educated residents.

On the other hand, too many of our rural communities in the less productive areas of the country have been "running downhill" in recent years because their agricultural resource base has been eroding away. This suggests that our approach to the question "To what extent should we conserve?" must employ the scientific knowledge and the intelligent foresight that are now available. At the same time we need to be discriminating. In some rough sort of way we must consider the cost of maintaining or rebuilding our natural-resource assets against the value of the resource conserved. Thus a farm family may have to choose between, on the one hand, using income to purchase lime, fertilizer, and grass seed and giving up income from a field for a year or two and, on the other hand, sending a son or daughter to high school or college that year. There is no ready solution when confronted with such a set of alternatives.

Actually, in most of the United States, farm families acquainted with modern methods by making slightly larger current investments can combine soil conservation with increased farm income. This is demonstrated in the current moderately successful educational and technical assistance programs carried on by the Extension Service and the Soil Conservation Service. Probably as many as two-thirds or three-fourths of our farm families could adopt soil conservation practices which would both conserve and rebuild their soil resources and increase their farm income within a few years. Yet there is a limit to which farm families can afford to go in maintaining and building up the soil and forestry assets on their farms. The limit is reached quickly on rented farms where the families have short-time leases or on heavily mortgaged farms. It is also reached rather quickly in the areas of scant and undependable rainfall, where it is not possible to practice a rotation of cultivated and close growing crops.

When considering the extent to which conservation should be encouraged, the social responsibility of farm leaders appears to take two forms. First, enlightened farm leaders are working for an improvement in the institutional arrangements involved in leasing farms and in extending credit on agricultural land to the end that the family operating the farm will have an interest in maintaining the farm's soil and other resources. The goal here is to achieve a situation where the farm will be operated in a manner comparable to that of a farm operated by a debt-free owner.

Second, farm leaders clearly want to encourage conservational systems of farming to the extent that they are consistent with the farm families' goal of increased income from the farm. As mentioned earlier, there is opportunity for much improvement in this matter on up to three-fourths of our farms.

To push conservation beyond this point in most cases is to ask farm families and communities to revalue their various goals of economic activity. To ask farmers to conserve or build up their soil to the point where the costs will not be covered by additional income in the near future or by the increased value of the farm if it were sold, is to ask farmers to make a gratuitous donation to the community.

There are, however, exceptional cases where soil erosion results in social costs greater than the losses of the farm owners. Where it can be clearly established that the community would benefit from a higher degree of conservation than is profitable for the owners and renters on the farms, the community finds it desirable to offer economic incentives for achieving the desired level of conservation.

Local farm leaders' responsibility in this field is both to help the community in determining the magnitude of the social costs involved as a result of current farming practices and to assume leadership in developing economic incentives for changes in practices commensurate with the gains which would flow to the community.

WHAT ARE THE APPROPRIATE METHODS?

Our progress to date in achieving better land use and more conservational systems of farming has been the result of three loosely related Government programs: education carried on by the Federal-State Extension Service; technical assistance furnished by the Soil Conservation Service; and payments for soil conservation practices, administered by the former Production and Marketing Administration, now by the Agricultural Program Service of the Commodity Stabilization Service. In each of the past several years the coordination and integration of these three programs has improved. Little progress has been made, however, in improving the institutional arrangements for leasing farm land and for extending credit under conditions which will encourage conservation farming practices. Although making payments for the performance of specified conservation practices has been continued for nearly twenty years, there is wide disagreement as to its effectiveness in achieving increased conservation. An important social responsibility of farm leaders is that of helping the public reach an intelligent decision regarding how much emphasis to place on each of these three methods of advancing conservation in the years ahead.

In addition to these three methods one other is available. This is the use of the "police power." Legislation in many of the states permits the local soil conservation districts to invoke land-use regulations, prohibiting the land users from engaging in specified practices detrimental to the community. European countries have made use of the police power rather extensively to control forestry practices, but little use has been made of the police power to conserve soil and forestry resources in the United States. It does not appear likely that this method will be used extensively in the near future, although it has found some favor as a method of obtaining uniform land use practices in Western areas suffering from severe wind erosion.

In this matter of appropriate methods for promoting increased soil conservation it is fruitless to argue that one is superior to all others.

To the extent that soil resources are not being conserved at a profitable level by current farming practices it would appear that educational programs should be sufficient. Yet the technical-assistance programs of the Soil Conservation Service have demonstrated their worth in almost every community in the United States. Payments for specified practices have resulted in their adoption on many farms on which they would not have been undertaken otherwise because of lack of ready cash. The question which is the most effective or the most economical combination of these three approaches will be answered differently as the public becomes more conservation conscious.

Theoretically, if the public fully appreciated the importance and value of conservational systems of farming, credit and leasing arrangements would be adapted to need and the normal economic incentives in our private enterprise system would result in greatly improved farm practices. Farm leaders realize, however, that farmers are not perfect "economic men." Farming practices that may provide economic returns sometime in the future all too often are neglected even though they will be profitable. Somehow positive social and economic forces must be built up in the community to supplement the normal functioning of our private enterprise system in this area if a desirable level of conservation is to be achieved and maintained. In a broad sense this is the social responsibility of local, state, and national farm leaders in the field of soil, water, and forestry conservation on privately-owned farm lands.

RESPONSIBILITIES OF PUBLIC OWNERSHIP

Over half of the land in the eleven Western states is in public rather than private ownership and hence directly subject to control in the public interest. This is in sharp contrast to the indirect methods required where the land is in private ownership. These public lands are generally unsuited for crops and for the most part are inferior grazing and forestry lands. Surely there should be no problem in conserving these low-valued natural resources. Yet a student of Western land use as recently as 1950 wrote:

In the arid Western part of the United States we face a test of wisdom and leadership. . . . This test will determine whether we can learn to use the resources of arid lands without destroying them, or . . . shall fall victim to the errors that have overtaken the peoples of arid lands, without exception, in the older countries of the world. . . .[2]

Actually, the conservation problems are fully as pressing on these public lands as on privately-owned farms and ranches. Some would say they are even more pressing. The urgency of the conservation problem on public lands is due to several factors. The high mountain lands of the West, largely in national forests which make up 20 per cent of the area, originate 80 per cent of the water yield so essential for urban development and farm-land irrigation. The scant and uncertain rain and snowfall make restoration of vegetation exceptionally difficult once it has been destroyed by overgrazing or overlogging.

Moreover, administration of public lands in a democracy is responsive to the will of people, usually the people most immediately and vitally affected by administrative actions. Hence the administrative actions on management policies tend to reflect the short-range, immediate objectives of the local people rather than the broader interest of the entire public. In this respect the controlling motives are similar to those of private land owners and the same need exists for education of the local people regarding conservation objectives.

In this setting, national and some state farm leaders have a special responsibility with respect to conservation of resources on public lands. In view of the current agitation for the return of many of these lands to private ownership, farm leaders should determine whether or not conditions have changed since the lands were placed in public ownership. The commonly accepted idea that public ownership assures management policies in the public interest needs correction. Leadership is needed in developing a better basis for determining the true or full public interest with respect to use and conservation of the resources of these relatively new arid lands in our Western states. Perhaps it is too much to expect complete agreement on desirable management policies for our publicly-owned lands, but surely intelligent farm leaders can do much to reconcile current conflicts regarding such policies by getting agreement on the results to be expected from specific policies.

[2] Mont. H. Saunderson, *Western Land and Water Use* (Norman, Oklahoma: University of Oklahoma Press, 1950), p. 43.

FLOOD PREVENTION A NEW CHALLENGE

Devastating floods in several midwestern states in recent years increased interest in flood-prevention and control activities to the extent that new legislation was enacted in 1954 by the 83rd Congress. The major flood-control work in this country has been carried on by the Army Corps of Engineers. They have built large flood-control dams and water-holding levees on many of our important rivers.

More recently the Soil Conservation Service, in cooperation with local watershed groups, has undertaken upstream flood-prevention activities. These activities include the construction of small water-holding dams in upper watershed waterways and programs to encourage shifts in land use which reduce water run-off. The public demand for increased flood-prevention activities of this type led to the new 1954 legislation mentioned above. Under this new legislation local watershed groups are encouraged to organize and request Federal assistance in undertaking flood-prevention activities.

At the present time a number of pilot watershed programs are in progress. The ultimate cost of carrying forward this attack on our flood problems will be formidable, even though spread over many years. A complete flood-prevention program for the United States along the lines now under way in these pilot watersheds would cost around $50 billion at current price levels.

In view of the potential magnitude of this relatively new undertaking, farm leaders' informed judgments will be of strategic importance in evaluating the alternative flood-prevention techniques. Unquestionably we have done too little in the way of flood prevention in the past. It would not be surprising, however, if sometime in the future we discover that we have overcorrected our past mistakes. Farm leaders must guard against spending money on flood-prevention activities of dubious value. With the enthusiasm for flood-prevention work which is sweeping the country today, farm leaders can alert the country to action in this field. Indeed, farm leaders will be called on to assist local watershed-sponsoring groups in setting up effective organizations and cooperative arrangements with Federal agencies which will result in maximum flood prevention per dollar spent.

PART II

Farm Leadership in Action

11

Farmers' Organizations

We turn now from a consideration of farmers' continuing social and economic problems to a description and analysis of farmers' organized efforts to deal with them. And, since organized groups acquire distinctive characteristics as a result of the environmental influences prevailing in their early years, we should look briefly at the earlier organization efforts.

Farmers organize to attain goals which they have been unable to attain by individual action. In early Colonial times they organized for mutual protection against Indian raids; to improve the schools for their children; to influence plantings, marketings, and prices of tobacco; to push inflationary schemes in periods of deflation; and to get local roads and canals built.

In the early period of statehood, and as new states were gradually added, farmers acted together to oppose the chartering of a United States Bank, to support currency expansion, to support public land disposal direct to settlers, and to improve prices and markets for their farm products. Largely because of difficulties of communication and transportation, farmers' protest movements in these early periods seldom resulted in formal farmers' organizations. Such agricultural societies as existed in these earlier years were concerned primarily with the promotion of agricultural arts and their leadership was in the hands of statesmen, scientists, nature lovers, and college professors rather than in the hands of active, practical farm operators. Most states had one or more of these agricultural societies in the early 1800s and they were the forerunners of our state departments of agriculture rather than of our current general farmers' organizations.

From the period beginning about 1870 to the present time farmers have joined together much more frequently and for longer periods of time than in earlier years in widespread protest and "trust busting" movements. There were good reasons for the increased protest activities of farmers after 1870. In the first place they were shifting rapidly from a largely handicraft, self-sufficing type of farming toward mechanized production for commercial markets. Fluctuating prices for their products resulted in new economic pressures on farm families. At the same time, new transportation and industrial systems were in a formative stage and in the absence of state and Federal regulations these new corporations often engaged in highly discriminatory practices.

Farmers' organizations with fraternal and social programs such as the Grange became deeply involved in protest movements regarding railroad rates and practices, monopolies in fence manufacturing, and malpractices of industrial groups. During this period farmers formed a number of new organizations for the purpose of improving their economic position, by organizing their own processing and equipment manufacturing companies, by organizing cooperative marketing agencies, and in a few cases through state ownership and operation of processing plants, banks, and rural credit agencies. The most prominent of these farmers' organizations in the period 1870 to 1910, besides the National Grange, were the Farmers Alliance, the Farmers' Wheel, the Farmers Union, and the American Society of Equity.

It was largely the militant action of the farmers in the Grange and in other allied organizations in the seventies that led to state regulation of the railroads and of monopolies, particularly in the Midwest states.

Economic conditions following World War I, including the sharp deflation in 1920-21 and the continued low prices for farm products relative to the prices of manufactured products, stimulated and sustained further farmer protest movements. These were participated in by the older Grange and the Farmers Union, as well as the newly-organized American Farm Bureau Federation and by smaller farmers' organizations such as the Missouri Farmers Association. Throughout the entire interwar period of the 1920s and the 1930s these general farmers' organizations devoted a great deal of their effort to promotion of specific legislative programs to improve farm prices and incomes relative to other groups in society.

TRADE ASSOCIATION FARM GROUPS

Not all farmer organizations have had legislative programs for the improvement of farmers' incomes and living standards as their primary objective. Beginning with the agricultural societies mentioned earlier which led to the formation of state departments of agriculture, farmers and people with specific farming interests have organized a wide variety of associations, similar to the nonfarm trade association groups. These include livestock breed-improvement associations, field crop-improvement associations, cattle feeders, lamb feeders, wool growers, dairymen, egg producers, broilermen, fruit producers, vegetable producers, and many smaller units within these larger organizations or associations.

These groups usually started with technical-improvement goals. They sponsored competitive exhibits at local and state fairs. They held educational meetings on improved production and marketing practices. For the most part, these associations remained aloof from the current social and economic issues. Members who felt strongly on the more general social and economic issues of the day were encouraged to take part in the activities of one of the more general farm organizations rather than to involve the small producer group in such controversial issues.

It is probable that the number of these farmers' organizations of the trade-association type is greater today than ever before. It is also probable that the number will continue to increase because of the continued increase in specialization and complexity in farm production each year. For example, we now have our hybrid seed corn growers and our inbred and crossbred hog producers, each group with its special interests. Also the marketing and processing of farm products continues to increase in complexity, so that each farm product has its special, yet continually changing, marketing problems.

While the leadership activities in these producers' groups of the trade-association type vary from group to group, they have a number of similarities. A large part of their activities are concerned with technical improvements in production and marketing which lead to increased efficiency in production and distribution. Few ethical or equity issues are encountered in this aspect of their programs.

However, increasingly in recent years these special producer groups have devoted a part of their activities to obtaining changes in government regulations in their favor. Wool producers have worked for increased tariffs and higher support prices on wool. Dairymen have worked for legislation to protect them from the competition of synthetic or substitute products and for restrictions on dairy imports. Cattle growers have been alert to maintain import restrictions on beef. Soybean producers have worked for government policies which would encourage larger exports of soybeans. A list of this sort could be extended almost indefinitely. In addition to the conflicting goals of the producers of different products, conflicts often occur between the goals of the producers of the same product in different geographic areas. A classic example of such conflict is the marketing of fluid milk in Southern and Eastern cities. Midwest milk producers are working for revisions in the urban milk market regulations that will permit them to sell their milk in these cities. Dairymen in territory adjacent to these cities prefer milk regulations that make it difficult for farmers to ship milk from Midwest areas.

The great number of specialized producers' organizations with partially conflicting goals often creates special problems for the general farmers' organizations. Most farmers who are members of a general farm organization such as the Farm Bureau, the Grange, or the National Farmers Union are also members of one or more of these special commodity groups. Usually their immediate economic interests are more closely identified with the programs of the special commodity groups of which they are members than with the program of the general organization. For this reason most of the changes in the regulations regarding the production and marketing of specific farm products are primarily sponsored by the special commodity groups. In the latter stages of such a campaign the general farmers' organizations may join in the sponsorship, but only after the goals of the special commodity group have been modified to meet most of the objections of other farm groups, or when the interests of several important commodity groups coincide. The general farm organizations can and do play an important role in broadening the perspective and goals of these special producers' organizations by meetings and discussions with them at the local, state, and national levels.

THE AMERICAN FARM BUREAU FEDERATION

Approximately 2.6 million farm families belong to one or another of the three leading general farmers' organizations today. Quite a number of farm families belong to two farm organizations.

The American Farm Bureau Federation is the youngest as well as the largest of these organizations. It reports a total membership of 1,609,461 farm families in 1954. The membership by states is shown in Table II. It was organized in 1920 as a federation of State Farm Bureaus, which in turn were federations of county farm bureaus. The county farm bureaus themselves had been organized by leading farmers as local sponsoring groups for the newly created Federal-State Extension (educational) Service. Although the founders of the American Farm Bureau were men primarily interested in promoting educational programs for farmers, they realized that their state and national organizations should have somewhat broader goals. They finally adopted a preamble which stated the objective of the national organization to be "to correlate and strengthen the Farm Bureaus of the several states and to promote, protect, and represent the business, social, economic, and educational interests of the farmers of the nation."[1] In the 1920s the American Farm Bureau actively supported the Agricultural Adjustment legislation, the creation of the Farm Credit Administration, and a number of related measures.

During World War II, the American Farm Bureau was active in protecting farmers' economic interests under price controls and allocations as well as in furnishing leadership to farmers in their war efforts. Throughout the Farm Bureau's life there has been strong support in the organization for expansion of research and educational programs for farmers and for state and local governmental programs in preference to centralized national programs. During the 1930s, however, the serious price declines and droughts caused the American Farm Bureau, as well as other organized farm groups, to turn to the national government for assistance. In 1947 a change in the presidency of the Farm Bureau occurred. People generally had become irritated with the wartime government controls and developed a strong desire to reduce national governmental activities as soon as possible. These two factors help to explain the emphasis in the American Farm Bureau in recent years on shifting to lower guaranteed price supports for farm products, on returning national governmental functions to the states and counties, and on increased research and education in lieu of direct-action programs.

Whereas in the early war years the American Farm Bureau took the leadership in pushing for higher government price supports, in the postwar years it has consistently advocated moderate reductions

[1] Theodore Saloutos and John D. Hicks, *Agricultural Discontent in the Middle West, 1900-1939* (Madison: University of Wisconsin Press, 1951), p. 267.

TABLE II. AMERICAN FARM BUREAU FEDERATION FAMILY
MEMBERSHIP BY STATES, 1954

State	Membership	State	Membership
Alabama	74,707	Nevada	1,365
Arizona	3,591	New Hampshire	5,136
Arkansas	55,881	New Jersey	7,910
California	59,363	New Mexico	8,116
Colorado	10,863	New York	77,157
Connecticut	5,529	North Carolina	71,056
Delaware	758	North Dakota	10,205
Florida	15,856	Ohio	48,917
Georgia	40,521	Oklahoma	40,006
Idaho	14,069	Oregon	7,036
Illinois	200,347	Pennsylvania	3,460
Indiana	116,688	Puerto Rico	5,104
Iowa	138,912	Rhode Island	286
Kansas	67,305	South Carolina	17,778
Kentucky	72,775	South Dakota	2,307
Louisiana	16,838	Tennessee	48,878
Maine	769	Texas	55,744
Maryland	10,023	Utah	7,524
Massachusetts	4,481	Vermont	8,267
Michigan	62,981	Virginia	12,678
Minnesota	32,920	Washington	4,844
Mississippi	46,125	West Virginia	3,588
Missouri	49,198	Wisconsin	34,506
Montana	2,972	Wyoming	7,533
Nebraska	16,588	Total Families	1,609,461

Source: American Farm Bureau Federation

in price-support levels in opposition to other political groups and farmers' organizations. In these more recent postwar years, the American Farm Bureau has continued to increase its membership each year, yet has consistently opposed government farm price-supports at the levels urged by many Congressmen. It has also opposed payments to farmers on the scale voted by Congress for the performance of soil-conservation practices on the ground that many payments were being made for temporary practices and for practices that had little conservation value. In this postwar period the American Farm Bureau has maintained a unique position for a special-interest group. In an over-all sense, its program has been one of asking government for less rather than more in the way of special economic assistance. It has adopted this program because its officers, backed up by a substantial majority of its members, believe that the farmers' incomes in the long run will be improved and the interests of equity better served if price-support levels and conservation payments are lower, with greater emphasis on educational procedures to help farmers increase their productive skills and managerial ability and on increased efforts in voluntary cooperative action.

THE NATIONAL GRANGE

The National Grange is the second largest general farmers' organization today. It reports a total membership of 847,419 in the spring of 1955. The Grange membership by states is shown in Table III. The early founders of the Order of the Patrons of Husbandry were interested in launching a farmers' fraternity similar in some respects to the successful Masonic Order. The Order of the Patrons of Husbandry was to be a nationwide fraternal organization of farmers stressing organization, education, cooperation, and legislation as a remedy for farm and national problems. The local branches of the Order were called Granges.

Reference has already been made to the way in which this organization in its early years in the 1870s had a wildfire growth as a protest movement against monopolistic practices of large corporations and especially against the arbitrary and discriminatory practices of the railroads. State regulatory legislation adopted in this period is still referred to as "Granger legislation." With the passage of regulatory legislation the farmers' protest movement and membership in the Grange declined sharply.

In the words of a past master of the National Grange:

The period of wildfire growth was followed by inevitable decline, but the Grange in a few years began to rebuild and to hold a firm place in national life and progress. . . . Fortunately the Grange placed emphasis on the soil, the forests and all our natural resources, but it is also believed that the farmer and his family were more important than the farm itself. The American way of farm life and the protection of the family-size farm became axiomatic with Grange growth and development. . . . The real power of the Grange is not found in its legislative or financial accom-

TABLE III. GRANGE MEMBERSHIP—BY STATES—SPRING 1955[1]

State	Membership	State	Membership
Arkansas	796	New Jersey	19,652
California	45,826	New York	129,378
Colorado	11,765	North Carolina	8,923
Connecticut	29,249	Ohio	174,602
Delaware	2,158	Oklahoma	2,087
Idaho	11,683	Oregon	28,670
Illinois	9,191	Pennsylvania	77,856
Indiana	5,550	Rhode Island	7,364
Iowa	2,828	South Carolina	4,544
Kansas	20,053	South Dakota	296
Maine	60,041	Tennessee	374
Maryland	3,053	Texas	2,085
Massachusetts	45,341	Vermont	18,050
Michigan	29,075	Virginia	1,657
Minnesota	3,335	Washington	50,365
Missouri	2,670	West Virginia	1,083
Montana	1,603	Wisconsin	2,834
Nebraska	1,987	Wyoming	1,270
New Hampshire	30,125	Total	847,419

[1] Note that Grange membership is on an individual rather than a family basis.
SOURCE: The National Grange.

plishments, but in the social and educational development of rural life. The effort to make the farm family a stronger unit, and rural communities more self-contained, laid the foundation for the great progress which started with the beginning of the Grange and covered the nation.[2]

Although the National Grange supported the McNary-Haugen bills in the early 1920s, it came out for an export debenture plan in 1926. It supported the Agricultural Adjustment legislation in the 1930s although it remained critical of some of its features. The Grange's continued criticism of the original parity formula was an important factor in the development of a modernized formula which was included in the Agricultural Act of 1948.

When the National Grange endorsed the export debentures plan it had in mind making the tariff effective for major farm crops where a part of the crop was exported each year. This was then

[2] Charles M. Gardner, *The Grange—Friend of the Farmer 1867-1947* (Washington, D. C.: The National Grange, 1950), p. xv.

followed by endorsement of two-price or multiple-price plans for commodities dependent on an export market. These plans, in recent years sometimes called self-financing, domestic parity plans, usually require the payment of parity prices for that part of the product which is used domestically while allowing exports to be made at world prices. This endorsement of domestic parity plans for export crops has continued until the present time.

In recent years, Grange membership has been largest in the Northwest, the Eastern corn belt, and the Northeast, with light membership in the South. In contrast, the Farm Bureau membership is heaviest in the Midwest and in the South. Perhaps because of this difference in membership distribution the Farm Bureau has been more active than the Grange in promoting freer international trade policies. In recent years the Grange, however, has likewise become a strong advocate of freer world trade.

The National Grange in the past 15 years has been taking a more active part in national legislative issues than at any time since the 1870s. In recent years the National Grange has also expanded its community improvement projects, youth programs, and activities for better farming and better living. A distinctive feature of the Grange program for several years has been its advocacy of self-financing two-price domestic parity measures for commodities having two or more relatively distinct markets. This is one of the ways in which the National Grange differs from both the Farm Bureau and the Farmers Union.

THE NATIONAL FARMERS UNION

The first State Farmers Union was organized in Texas in 1902 with a reported membership of 50,000. In the first decade of its life, the Farmers Union flourished primarily in the South, but after 1912 membership declined in the South and increased in the wheat-growing states where it is strongest today. The estimated family membership by states is shown in Table IV.

The Farmers Union was organized primarily to assist farmers in marketing and in obtaining better prices for their products, and to give them an opportunity for cooperation in the protection of their interests. In the early years of the organization it sponsored a movement to raise prices by withholding from the market one bale of cotton out of every five produced. It attempted to influence the

TABLE IV. NATIONAL FARMERS UNION ESTIMATED FAMILY
MEMBERSHIP BY STATES, 1955[1]

State	Membership	State	Membership
Arkansas	16,000	Oregon	3,000
Idaho	2,000	Pennsylvania	1,750
Illinois	6,000	Rocky Mountain	18,750
Indiana	7,200	(Colorado—Wyoming)	
Kansas	12,000	South Dakota	20,000
Michigan	4,300	Tennessee	1,200
Minnesota	4,000	Texas	4,800
Montana	16,250	Utah	5,000
Nebraska	17,500	Virginia	7,000
North Carolina	2,000	Washington	2,500
North Dakota	44,000	Wisconsin	14,000
Ohio	1,750	Other States	1,000
Oklahoma	52,000	*Total Families*	300,000

[1] Membership cards are issued to each dues paying member in the family. The voting membership for the calendar year 1954 was slightly in excess of 600,000.
SOURCE: National Farmers Union

price of cotton by advising its members to hold their crops until a certain price was reached and by conducting acreage-reduction campaigns. It recommended the building of cotton warehouses by county and local unions and it mobilized its power against the "tyrannical" Cotton Exchange. The state unions established business departments and sold their own cotton, went into the fertilizer business, purchased farm supplies, and performed many diverse business operations.

These early activities of the Farmers Union set a pattern which continues to be characteristic of it up to the present time. Much of the National Farmers Union strength in the last two decades has been the result of its efficiently operated grain elevators and related cooperative services in the Northwest and its cooperative livestock-marketing agencies in the Midwest.

Carl Taylor, a student of farmers' movements, wrote of the activities of the Farmers Union in its early years as follows:

It did not often deliver scathing tirades against "trusts, combines, and monopolies," as the Grangers, Wheelers, and Alliance men had, but it constantly took its stand in behalf of more equitable distribution of wealth; and [in the 1915-20 period] declared in favor of "government ownership or control of all natural resources; as minerals, oil, coal, phosphates, lime, building stone, timbers, and water powers." It also asked for a limitation on large holdings of land and government ownership of railroads. For the most part, however, this great farm organization, in the first twenty years of its existence, spent its major effort in a more or less systematic attack on the price and market problems of the farmer. . . .[3]

During the late 1920s and the 1930s the Farmers Union went through substantial reorganizations, particularly in relation to the business enterprises sponsored. Throughout this period it emphasized cooperative marketing, supported plans to put price floors under commodities, and endorsed parity and production control programs. Farmers Union from its earliest years differed from the Farm Bureau and the Grange in engaging in more informal cooperative activities with organized labor, in its greater emphasis on the problems of the small farmer, and in its advocacy of market reforms which often include greater government participation in production and marketing of farm products than the other farmer organizations were willing to endorse. This distinction is evident also in a review of its current program, which endorses farm price supports at 100 per cent of parity on all farm products up to a certain family-farm volume of production per farm. Supplies produced in excess of domestic market requirements would be channeled into the hands of needy people in this country, and in friendly countries by means of international agreements.

NATIONAL COUNCIL OF FARMER COOPERATIVES

In addition to the three general farm organizations, the National Council of Farmer Cooperatives actively promotes the interests of its members in the broader fields of agricultural and economic policy. It is an association of farmers' business organizations, members of which are farmer-owned and farmer-controlled cooperatives engaged in the marketing of agricultural commodities or the purchasing of essential farm production supplies.

This Council was established in 1929 in response to the need for

[3] Carl C. Taylor, *The Farmers Movement, 1620-1920* (New York: American Book Company, 1953), pp. 363-364.

a national association of farmer cooperatives which could act speedily and effectively in matters of national importance. It now has 116 direct and associate members, most of which are federated cooperatives. Through these federated cooperatives the Council actually represents approximately 5000 cooperatives which serve a membership of nearly 3 million.

While the Council is most directly concerned with matters affecting farmer cooperatives, its activities extend to broader fields. It serves as a forum and coordinating body through which its member organizations formulate policy and as an action agency through which efforts are made to implement these policies. The National Council works with the Congress and with administrative agencies of the government in formulating and carrying out agricultural and economic policies. It provides a means through which affiliates may be advised of developments which affect the farmers they serve, and joins with other farm organizations in the support of many policies.

The Council has seventeen commodity and functional divisions and functions on a divisional basis. Annual meetings of the Council's membership are held and it issues a number of publications each year, among which are the Annual Year Book, a weekly newsletter, and bulletins of a more specialized nature.

The Common Goals of the Farm Organizations

As is true of most special-interest groups, each of the farmers' organizations discussed in the preceding paragraphs believes that in carrying out its current program it is working to improve the equity position of its members. In a long-run setting, at least, each organization believes that its program will not only improve the economic position of its members but also increase the general welfare. All are concerned primarily with the welfare of the family-type farm. They believe in addition that only those individuals and groups that are reaping "unearned profits" or are benefiting from some "current racket" will fail to benefit from their programs.

Yet, as indicated earlier, differences exist between the programs of the three general farm organizations. The Farm Bureau believes that the private "free choice" economic system with a minimum of governmental interference will serve farmers' needs best. Beginning in the war years, in its view, government farm programs have been too extensive, and over the long run farmers will get more equitable treatment and improve their economic position if government farm programs are reduced.

On the other hand, Farmers Union believes that the present private-enterprise system, modified as it is by government farm programs, still leaves farmers in an inferior economic and social position as compared with other major groups in society. It favors having the government undertake additional activities to increase and stabilize farm incomes. In particular it believes farm price supports should be raised and extended to all important farm products.

While the general goals of the Grange are the same as those of the other farm organizations, its program is intermediate between the programs of the other two.

It is because the issues of how best to attain these goals have never been settled that these three general farmer organizations continue to champion different economic programs. Only by following the suggestions outlined in the chapters in Part I, which include continued research on the economic effects of specific policy measures, can progress be made in narrowing existing differences in program recommendations of the farmers' organizations.

INSTITUTIONAL CONTINUITY IN FARM ORGANIZATION

Institutional continuity is both a virtue and a handicap in social groups such as the farmers' organizations under discussion. The fact of continuity is well illustrated by the observations of a farm editor when each of the major farm organizations was asked by Secretary Benson to make a "grass roots" or widespread membership study of changes needed in existing farm legislation in 1953. The farm editor, in a conversation with the writer, predicted that the Farm Bureau members would endorse flexible price supports as the major change needed, the Grange members would urge the adoption of two-price plans, and the Farmers Union members would endorse "100 per cent of parity" price supports on an expanded list of products. Less than a year later, the reports and resolutions of these national farm organizations followed precisely the pattern predicted.

This incident highlights one of the great difficulties faced by all large social organizations in a rapidly changing environment. How can the organization achieve a sufficiently integrated set of procedures to function effectively on a specific issue and yet maintain sufficient flexibility to bring new insights to bear on new problems? The problem appears to become more serious as the organizations grow in size. Yet each of these farm organizations points with pride to its recent growth statistics.

Here is a problem that challenges the most competent farm leaders. Never before have the social and economic problems confronting farmers changed so rapidly as in recent years. Never before have farmers been so well organized. Can these large organizations of farmers keep up with the changing times? Can the membership educate or elect new officers rapidly enough to maintain an effective program of action focused on current problems?

Can the officers educate the membership with sufficient speed to assure their support of new policies when the events call for strong organization action along new lines? Officers are expected to understand issues more fully than their membership and problems are usually thought of in terms of membership educational programs. Yet in individual cases the cause-and-effect relationship may be reversed. Leaders concentrating their efforts on deep-rooted chronic problems may be slower than many of the members in coming to grips with new problems that arise out of our constantly changing environment.

It is encouraging to note that each of the farm organizations recognizes the vital importance of widespread membership participation in policy formulation and is expanding its efforts in this field. The newer and younger officers at the local levels are better trained than the officers they have replaced. The professional staffs of all the general farm organizations have been expanded as much as or more than the membership gains. With this strengthened organizational backing, farm leaders should be able to mobilize their increased memberships to meet new problems as they arise.

12

The Process of State Farm Leadership

In many ways the state general farm organizations play a larger role in our society than the national organizations. In each state where the general farm organization has a sufficiently large membership to finance a state office staff an active legislative program is carried on. In order to get a better firsthand picture of the leadership activities of the state presidents of these three organizations, the writer interviewed a substantial number of them in the winter of 1954-55.

A typical interview included such questions as these: whether the president's office (master in the case of the state Grange) was a full-time job; what activities took the largest share of the president's time and energy; what was the most important project or activity of the state organization in the last year or two; what aspects of the president's job gave the most satisfaction and which were most troublesome. The interview included also questions as to the unique contributions of the president to the organization and possible improvements in the programs of the state and national organizations.

The activities and general programs of the state heads of the three general farm organizations are determined in a roughly similar manner. Each state organization has an annual meeting of voting delegates from the organized counties and in some cases from local units in unorganized counties. These voting delegates elect a board of directors and other state officers. They also adopt a set of resolutions which the officers and the board of directors are instructed to implement insofar as possible in the following year. The voting delegates also take actions on "housekeeping" matters which set the limits on the duties and responsibilities of the officers. Within the limits of the often broadly phrased resolutions, the president in consultation with his board of directors has wide latitude in mobilizing the strength of his organization in support of or in opposition to specific proposals or policies.

The president of a state farm organization performs two different leadership functions in which his individual personality, character, knowledge, interests, and ethics have a great deal to do with the part his organization plays in society. As the most influential single member or officer in the organization, he directs the attention of the membership to problems and specific aspects of problems in such a way that even indirectly he influences the content of the resolutions which are adopted and the instructions given him by the delegate body. A number of the state presidents in the larger state organizations, however, deliberately stay away from all meetings of the resolutions committee in order to avoid the danger of influencing it unduly.

As the elected spokesman of the organization, the president is the organization's "field general" charged with planning and executing the strategy and public relations to implement the resolutions adopted by the voting delegates. It is in this role that the state president and other elected officers encounter the perennial question how to reconcile the responsibility of faithfully carrying out the instructions of the delegates and at the same time give intelligent leadership based on all the relevant facts and circumstances. To the extent that state officials promote an effective educational program, keeping channels of discussion and information open from members through to state officials, this problem tends to diminish.

STATE FARM BUREAU LEADERSHIP

Interviews with approximately half the state Farm Bureau presidents in December 1954 indicated that one of the most commonly held beliefs of these officers is that the role of centralized government in the economic life of the nation and in agriculture should be reduced. These state Farm Bureau leaders believe that in the long run farmers can best maintain a lively self-reliance, self-respect, and greater security on the farm through taking responsibility for more of their economic decisions regarding what to raise, how much, when to sell, etc., and by placing more reliance on working together with their neighbors in cooperatives and in general farm organizations. Several of them specifically mentioned activities directed toward this end as the most important aspect of their leadership duties at the present time. Others indicated concurrence in this view, but listed other activities as well.

From the standpoint of the present study, it is important to note that the reason for this widely held attitude was not primarily irritations with specific governmental activities in the field of agriculture. Their concern over excessive governmental direction of economic affairs was expressed in such broad terms as might have been used by many nonfarm people holding similar views. Furthermore, most of the presidents and the state Farm Bureaus are willing to give up a part of their present price guarantees and conservation payments, even though immediate farm incomes are somewhat lowered, in order to reduce governmental interference in agriculture. Their position on this fundamental issue is based on economic, ideological, and ethical considerations.

They do not believe that price guarantees at recent levels will increase farmers' income in the long run. They point out that markets are being lost and substitutes have been encouraged by recent price-support guarantees. Their desire to see governmental activities restricted has also another economic basis, the desire to have taxes reduced. Property, income, and excise taxes all spirit away their incomes and increase their business costs. Fewer governmental activities should permit reductions in taxes.

It is doubted, however, that the economic motive for desiring reduced centralized governmental activities is as strong among these Farm Bureau leaders as are two others which may be respectively classified as ideological and ethical. First, in their view, governmental activities, while they may confer temporary economic gains on large numbers of citizens, almost always restrict individual liberties. Farm Bureau leaders have developed, in recent years, a vivid picture of what the continuation of governmental trends of the past two decades may lead to in the way of restricted individual liberties. The ethical basis for their current position is the conviction that the individual's and the family's moral fiber is being undermined by these same aspects of the governmental assistance and economic-security programs which have come into existence in the last twenty years.

Variations among States

As might be expected, there was a wide variation in the major activities of the Farm Bureau reported in the past year in the different states. Two leaders reported work on the state legislative reapportionment as their most important activity. Several reported as their major undertaking projects designed to increase member activity in policy formulation. In a leading dairy state a major activity in 1954 was educating the members to accept willingly a lower support price on dairy products. As a result, the voting delegates in this state at their annual meeting in December endorsed the lower dairy price supports as being in their long-time interest. This is in contrast to the actions of the National Milk Producers Federation (many of whose members are also Farm Bureau members) and other groups of dairy producers who at their 1954 annual meetings passed resolutions asking for higher-level supports.

One state Farm Bureau president reported a successful campaign to reorganize the state department of agriculture as the major 1954 project. Several mentioned their educational work on price-support programs as a major activity in recent years. Broadening the tax base to relieve the load of property taxes, securing improvements in the school program, promoting highway construction in financing, and developing a sound water conservation policy were listed as other important activities of one or more state Farm Bureaus.

Two of the Midwest states may be cited for notably broad programs of state Farm Bureaus. In addition to reporting several of the issues mentioned above, they reported also that their state legislative programs included increased appropriations for state institutions, increased state aid for schools, legislative authority for rural zoning, an egg-grading law, and in one of the states the establishment of a veterinary college.

Satisfactions in Farm Bureau Leadership

The first state Farm Bureau president interviewed reported getting most satisfaction out of seeing leadership develop in the new men taken on the various county and state boards from time to time. A state Farm Bureau president for ten years, in a state with a large membership, reported that he took great pride in and satisfaction from the progress that had been made in making the state organization more responsive to the thinking of the membership. This is a major project of his state office and he looks forward to further improvements in this area.

Several state presidents expressed similar views both as to their greatest satisfaction derived from leadership activities and as to their efforts to get the members to take more interest in the affairs of the state Farm Bureau. Just as there was marked unanimity regarding the urgency of reversing recent trends in government, there was an equally widespread belief that increased educational work with the members and a program to achieve increased membership participation in policy formulation should be given high priority.

A president in one of the weaker states said he got most satisfaction out of seeing more member participation in the affairs of the Farm Bureau. Another found most satisfaction in helping people unify their purposes through group activities. A third gave as his chief ground for satisfaction just working with people—helping them achieve their purposes.

Several state presidents expressed some variation of the theme that they got most satisfaction out of helping farmers to present a united front and helping them to improve rural conditions. One of the more eloquent presidents reported that his greatest satisfaction was "in helping build in the minds and hearts of people, through Christian ideals and democratic processes, a great unified voice for agriculture which will provide a stabilizing influence for farm people and for the entire economy."

Major Problems

Several state presidents indicated that their major problems lay in the same areas as their major satisfactions. To make the state organization more responsive to the membership and to get the membership to take a more active part in policy formulation appears to be their major problem. Others expressed a somewhat similar concern when they said their greatest problem was the members' lack of understanding and unreadiness to use information. The president in one of our highly industrialized states reported his greatest problem as getting recognition of the importance of agriculture in the state; another mentioned improving public relations. One president thought that his greatest problem in the past two years was to get effective action in stabilizing the value of the dollar.

Special Contributions of Individuals

Each state president was asked to reflect a moment and then indicate what he thought was his special contribution during the period he had been president. A representative sample of the replies follows: developing depth in both staff and leaders; sharing the responsibilities of decision-making with more people; selecting and appointing capable persons to manage business subsidiaries, to chair the important Farm Bureau committees, and to act as coordinators among them. Some listed such contributions as bringing farm and producer groups in the state into a general farm organization; departmentalizing the work and assigning definite responsibilities; financing cooperatives on a sound basis; and getting people to understand each other's problems and to work together. One new president reported that attendance at and participation in Farm Bureau meetings, thus getting familiar with Farm Bureau ideals in the years before he became president, had more influence on his thinking than he as president would have on the Farm Bureau organization.

STATE GRANGE LEADERSHIP

Interviews with over half the state masters of the National Grange left the writer with a feeling of wide differences in major interests and purposes among the various state Granges and their masters. In New England, where many of the state Granges are relatively strong, the social and fraternal interests appear to be dominant in several of the states. On the other hand, the strong state Granges of the far West appear to be most interested in supporting legislative programs dealing with rural problems.

While a number of state Granges have such membership service programs as affiliated automobile, accident, health, fire, and life insurance companies, no state Granges, except in the state of Washington, have affiliated cooperative marketing and farm supply cooperatives comparable to the affiliated cooperatives of the Farm Bureaus in the Midwest states. In many cases, because of the small membership, the state master is on a part-time basis and serves entirely without salary. In a number of cases unpaid state masters find it possible to devote a large amount of time to state Grange work because they are partially retired from active farming or affiliated business activities.

State masters of the National Grange may hold views relative to government and economic life similar to those expressed by state Farm Bureau presidents; but in the brief interviews other aspects of their leadership activities seemed more important to them. In recent years the National Grange has been stressing the opportunities for reinvigorating local Granges by the adoption of community service projects. The cash awards for outstanding community-service projects made possible by the cooperation of the Sears-Roebuck Foundation also added interest to this Grange activity and contributed to the high place it held among all Grange activities in many states. When asked, "What was the most important activity of your state Grange in the past year?" many state masters gave first place to support of community service projects by the local Granges.

Two of the states reported that their most active projects in the past year or two were campaigns in their states to get legislative authorization for legal separation of the Federal-State Extension Service from the state and county Farm Bureaus. This legal separation has now (1955) been achieved in all states except Illinois, Iowa, and New York, and similar action is now in process in these states. Several states reported support of youth activities and juvenile Granges as among their most important current activities. Several state masters gave first importance to projects to get increased local Grange participation in policy formulation and the development of the state legislative program.

Almost every state master mentioned a specific item of state or national legislation as typical of Grange interests in legislative programs. In one state it was development of the St. Lawrence Waterway; in another, farm-to-market roads; in another, soil and water conservation; and in one state revision of the state tax laws had high priority. The Western states placed a high priority on land, water, and power-resource development in their Grange programs.

State Masters' Problems

Perhaps because Grange membership is smaller than Farm Bureau membership, but also because many members join on account of their interest in the ritual and fraternal associations provided by the Order of the Patrons of Husbandry, lack of local interest in state and national legislative programs is a greater problem for masters of state Granges than for state Farm Bureau presidents. Several state masters reported that their greatest problem was to find enough time to carry on the administrative, public relations, and leadership duties of the office on a part-time, nonpaid basis.

Several state masters listed the selection of committee chairmen and staff as their most important problems. In some cases the problem was stated in terms of the difficulty of getting the best qualified members to accept the responsibility of committee chairmanships. One state master gave credit for much of the membership growth in his state in recent years to the outstanding work of his assistant in charge of home economics activities.

None of the state masters or state Farm Bureau presidents reported encountering problems arising out of conflicts between the interests or goals of their organization and the interests of the economy as a whole. When asked questions in this area their replies indicated that they believed their resolutions' committees successfully blocked special-interest proposals. They believe that only those proposals which are in the general interest receive official endorsement. This is a belief shared by the leaders in many other interest groups.

Greatest Satisfactions in Grange Leadership

Grange leaders are individuals who enjoy the fellowship of fraternal association with Grangers. State masters often reported "working with fine people" as the greatest satisfaction obtained from their job. Several reported that their greatest source of satisfaction was work with the youth groups in the Grange, while two mentioned participation in and improvement of the ritualistic work.

In the states with the largest membership and the most active legislative programs, the state masters indicated that their greatest satisfaction came from helping farm families accomplish their objectives through organized strength in the legislative halls and committee rooms.

Special Contributions of Individuals

State masters' answers to the question concerning their special contribution to the Grange program differed almost as widely as human personalities differ. One reported that he believed if he made any unique contribution it was his ability (and luck) in appointing outstanding staff and committee chairmen. He credited the success of the Grange program in his state to these individuals and said that if a state master can only get competent staff and committees he is assured of a strong Grange program.

Two of the state masters mentioned their public relations work as their special contribution. Both men thought the public relations responsibilities and opportunities associated with their position were an unusual challenge. They liked public relations work to which more than half their time is devoted.

In several states where the Grange has only a small membership, the state masters believed their major contributions to be leadership activities with the local Granges to get them to adopt more active community service programs and other activities which would stimulate increase in membership. It seemed evident to the writer that leadership-selection processes in the state Granges usually resulted in the election of a state master who had a strong sense of social responsibility and a desire to be of service to his fellow men. Of the thirty-seven states with organized state Granges only ten have masters serving on a full-time basis and paid a full-time salary.

STATE FARMERS UNION LEADERSHIP

Interviews with fifteen of the seventeen state presidents of Farmers Union in March 1955 impressed the writer with the great uniformity in idealism and the prevalence of a substantial missionary spirit among state presidents in the Farmers Union. In contrast to the concern of state Farm Bureau presidents because of excessive governmental control over economic matters, the Farmers Union state presidents believe that their organization has a great mission to perform in giving farmers an opportunity to participate actively in policy formulation in our "legislative economy," a term used by Farmers Union to indicate that all parts of the economy today are vitally affected by legislative action. Their primary purpose appears to be that of carrying forward a legislative program for the protection of the family farm.

One of the state presidents said that the goal of his state organization was to build membership on the basis of citizen responsibility in a "legislative economy." This particular state president, after developing a large, outstanding, successful farming operation in the past twenty-seven years, is now devoting his time and energies to Farmers Union activities. He believes that unless a family farm program such as the Farmers Union advocates is adopted we are in danger of losing the rural institutions which have permitted American agriculture to become the most productive and efficient in the world.

The state presidents of the Farmers Union, with few exceptions, believed that operators of family farms should be assured 100 per cent of parity prices for their products. This is an important part, they believe, of an over-all program to protect family farms. Several state presidents said corporations such as the public utilities, the banking institutions, and many industrial corporations maintained lobbyists who protected their interests in the state and national capitals. They thought of Farmers Union as an organization with a "liberal" program to checkmate the selfish activities of these lobbyists and to give the family farmer a measure of political and economic power at conference tables where legislative strategy and administrative decisions are formulated.

New State Organizations

As a result of reorganizations in the national offices and of discontent among farmers as farm incomes have declined since 1951, Farmers Union is increasing its state organizations at the present time. Although the total growth in membership in 1954 was less than the total growth in Farm Bureau membership, percentagewise Farmers Union growth was far greater. Many states with only a few thousand members increased their membership substantially. For example, in 1954, Farmers Union was chartered as a new state organization with 5000 or more members in Illinois, Indiana, Utah, and Virginia. Under new leadership the state organization in Texas also has taken a new lease on life in the last year or two.

With increased assistance from national headquarters in recent years almost every state with a Farmers Union organization is engaged in an active campaign sharply to increase membership. Almost without exception this was the major activity of state organizations in 1954. With guidance and assistance from national headquarters, the state organizations are setting up and expanding business services for members similar to those which have been outstandingly successful in such states as the Dakotas, Montana, and Minnesota.

In 1955 the National Farmers Union announced plans to develop potash deposits which it owns in New Mexico. With additional funds anticipated from this source, it has launched a ten-year expansion program to achieve a goal of an active Farmers Union with affiliated business services in each of the forty-eight states.

Importance of National Legislative Program

Only a few state Farmers Unions, such as those in North and South Dakota, Montana, Nebraska, Oklahoma, and Arkansas have had a large enough membership over a period of years to develop substantial state legislative programs. In the other states and even in these states, active interest and membership are maintained largely on the basis of the organization's national legislative program. Both the national and the state Farmers Union spend a large part of their budgets on research and educational work. They try to keep their members informed on national legislative developments and stimulate them to express their views by passing appropriate resolutions at the meetings of their locals.

Satisfactions of State Leaders

There was substantial uniformity in the answers of state Farmers Union presidents to the question, "What aspects of your job as state president give you the most satisfaction?" The first one interviewed replied: "I get the greatest satisfaction out of watching the development of folks when they begin to participate in the Farmers Union program. Give them any chance at all and it's wonderful to see people develop." Another said he came from a poor background but had had several years' experience as a state legislator. He is impressed with the injustices in our present economic system and gets greatest satisfaction out of helping in a program to inform citizens of their duties and responsibilities in a democratic society —and in seeing people respond to his efforts in this field. Others expressed similar sentiments in terms of helping in "a great liberal program" and giving farmers an opportunity to reason together with open minds regarding the solution of economic and social problems confronting them.

Major Problems

State Farmers Union presidents with the missionary spirit mentioned earlier said that their most frustrating experience was the complacency of farm people, especially when times are not bad.

They find it difficult to understand why it is so hard to arouse and maintain the average farm family's interest in their legislative program and in the affiliated cooperative services. One of the newer Farmers Union presidents, in a state where membership has expanded rapidly in recent years, mentioned that one of his problems was to keep the officers of the locals aware of their social responsibility in its broader context.

Contributions of Individuals

Few of the state presidents in Farmers Union have held their present positions for more than five years, and most have been primarily occupied in recent years with membership expansion campaigns; hence their distinctive characteristics as farm leaders were not so readily apparent as in the case of the state officers of the other farm organizations. However, two of the most successful leaders mentioned their ability to get people to work together and their ability to coordinate various activities and groups as their special contribution. Others mentioned, as perhaps their major contribution, their belief in the "rightness" of the Farmers Union program and their willingness to take an unpopular position in support of this program.

SIMILARITIES IN STATE FARM ORGANIZATION PROGRAMS

There are many similarities in the state programs of the three general farm organizations in the mid-1950s. The state Farm Bureaus, already counting a majority of the farm families in their membership in several states, are continuing a steady membership growth. For the most part they are providing affiliated cooperative insurance and cooperative marketing and farm supply services to help maintain membership. These affiliated cooperative business activities are growing in importance every year.

State Farmers Unions are now engaged in a widespread membership expansion program with plans to set up similar cooperative business services for their members. The business activities of the state and national Farmers Unions are a major responsibility of the state and national officers, especially now that the national organization is developing its potash deposits. In several states the Grange is engaged in an expansion of affiliated insurance services. But for the most part state Grange activities in the mid-1950s are giving increased emphasis to the community service projects of the local Granges as a means of encouraging increased membership activity.

Both the state Farm Bureaus and the state Farmers Unions are increasing their informational and educational budgets and are making an active effort to get more membership participation in the formulation and direction of state and national programs.

The three farm organizations differ primarily in their legislative programs for achieving their common goals. The nature and extent of these differences will be developed in the chapters that follow.

13

Farmers' County Organizations

National and state organizations must have an underpinning of county and local units. In this chapter we shall describe and analyze the organization and activities of the local and county units of the three contemporary general farm organizations, the Farm Bureau, the Grange, and the Farmers Union.

Local Farm Bureaus

The Farm Bureau with its 1,609,461 members has by far the largest number of active local units. In most northern states the rural township or town is the local Farm Bureau unit. In the South the community, which may be smaller than a township, is more often the local unit of the Farm Bureau. The activities of the township farm bureaus are largely educational and social. They sponsor 4-H club work for both boys and girls, rural women's educational clubs, Extension Service projects, and similar activities.

Although there are wide variations within and among states in the vigor and the activities of township farm bureaus they continue to emphasize educational and social activities in their monthly or less frequent meetings. Since rural women have more interest in and time for social meetings than rural men, the wives in Farm Bureau member families often have more active local organizations than the men. In recent years many of the township units, in addition to their educational and youth activities, have undertaken community improvement projects and spend several meetings each year in the study of policy issues.

Several state Farm Bureaus have well-organized education departments which sponsor and service, with discussion materials, community or township groups which meet monthly and discuss public problems. Probably the Ohio Farm Bureau is the leader in this activity, with about 1500 local groups meeting monthly and reporting their views to the state office. The Michigan Farm Bureau is another leader in this field, with 1200 local groups meeting monthly and reporting their views. In Ohio and several other states the discussion topics are selected by majority vote and each month all groups discuss the same topic. Among the topics scheduled for discussion in Ohio in 1955 were: Our milk problems; Paying for our highways; Can we build better farm-city relations?; What do city workers and farmers have in common? This type of activity is recognized as highly desirable and additional states are adopting activities of this type each year.

The county Farm Bureau is directed by a county president and board of directors. The board of directors is usually elected from the different communities in the county; where the county is organized on a township basis the township president is a member of the county board. The variation in county Farm Bureau activities is almost as wide as the variation in the activities of local units. Each county having a substantial number of Farm Bureau members is organized and has a set of officers. The county Farm Bureaus sponsor 4-H club work and other youth activities, agricultural educational activities, and perhaps one or more rural social events. Whereas the local unit usually has a social and educational program, the county Farm Bureau functions primarily administratively as the local policy formulation unit. Annual county membership meetings are usually held. The work of the county Farm Bureau is performed by its officers, on a voluntary (nonpaid) basis.

County and state Farm Bureaus also may sponsor county and state-wide sports festivals, talent finds, public speaking contests, and other youth activities.

Many state and county Farm Bureaus now have affiliated cooperative insurance, marketing, and supply companies. Members' savings in utilizing these cooperative services are often greater than the membership fees. Membership campaigns, affiliated cooperative business undertakings, and sponsorship of local rural improvement projects take up much of the time of the county Farm Bureau Boards and their other elected officers. In more recent years many county Farm Bureaus have appointed resolutions or legislative committees and these committees have developed resolutions regarding rural life matters for consideration by the members at their annual county meetings. Local papers usually publish a part or all of the resolutions adopted by the county Farm Bureau, but the major purpose of passing the resolutions is to inform the state federation of the position of the county membership on the more important current issues.

LOCAL AND COUNTY GRANGES

The National Grange has an organization only roughly similar to the American Farm Bureau; there are many differences. Farmers become members of the National Grange by joining the local fraternal Order of the Patrons of Husbandry. This local group is a subordinate grange in the national organization. It usually assumes the local community name such as the Hazel Dell Grange. Subordinate Granges meet on the average twice a month throughout the year.

The county or regional organization of subordinate Granges is called a Pomona Grange; e.g., the Franklin County Pomona Grange. Pomona Granges report to the state Grange which simply adopts the name of the state where it is located. The National Grange is now made up of thirty-seven state Granges. Perhaps because it is a fraternal organization with a special ritual, Grange members are primarily interested in the activities of their local or subordinate Granges. In more recent years many local Granges have functioned primarily as the rural community social organization. Grange women often form Home Economics clubs within the Grange which are extremely active. The Pomona, state, and National Granges have their home economics committees which organize program materials, sponsor sewing, cooking, and baking contests, and otherwise give leadership to the local Grange home economics clubs. (Several state masters have given the home economics program a major share of the credit for the growth of Grange membership and activities in their states in recent years.)

The local and Pomona Granges sponsor youth activities, including Boy and Girl Scouts and Juvenile Granges for the youngsters in the Grange families. Children may become members of the Order of the Patrons of Husbandry at the age of 14. Youth programs, including public speaking contests, Scout programs, camping, and many other activities, help these younger Grange members to develop into useful citizens. In many subordinate Granges the officers organize Juvenile Granges for the children under 14 to let them have the experience of electing officers and conducting Juvenile Grange meetings, and above all to give them an opportunity to become familiar with Grange ideals at this early age. One state Grange Master made the observation that if every child could have two years of experience in a Juvenile Grange, juvenile delinquency would cease to be a problem.

Local or subordinate Granges, as well as local Farm Bureaus, have often taken the leadership in community activities, such as getting hot lunches served in the schools, establishing a rural church, or initiating a community recreation program. In recent years, with the cooperation of the Sears-Roebuck Foundation, the National Grange has sponsored an annual Community Service Contest. In 1954, 3100 out of the 7200 subordinate Granges in the United States were actively competing for the $15,000 grand prize and the many smaller prizes offered in that contest. The 1954 winner of the grand prize of $15,000 was the Arcadia Grange of Lexington, North Carolina. Services totaling in excess of 5340 hours of donated time by the members included construction of a community center, assistance to a cancer clinic, and health and nursing programs, a mailbox-improvement project, inspection of 150 homes for fire hazards, and a weed-control campaign. Each subordinate Grange that enters the contest selects its own community service project or projects.

The extent to which local and Pomona Granges formulate positions on policy issues and attempt to influence social action varies greatly from Grange to Grange and from state to state. In the states of Oregon and Washington, where the members are generally aware of the resource development problems, many of the local Granges take positions on power and irrigation development issues and related matters. At the other extreme, the members of many of the subordinate Granges in New England are rural or suburban residents who earn their living in nonfarm occupations and have little interest in farm issues. While local, state, and national issues concerning rural life may be taken up in the typical meeting of a subordinate or Pomona Grange, the lecturer, an elected Grange member who has charge of organizing the program for regular Grange meetings, more often selects other subjects. He often selects subjects dealing with Grange history and ideals, or with general historical or national events; or it may be a religious topic. Only when the local membership gets aroused over local, state, or national issues are they made the subject of discussion at the regular subordinate Grange meetings.

Leadership in both the state Granges and the National Grange in recent years has given increased attention to the formulation and carrying out of legislative programs in the states and in the nation. As a part of this increased concern with legislative programs, Pomona and subordinate Granges are urged by the state Granges to give increased attention to rural-life issues which are currently the subject of legislative action.

LOCAL AND COUNTY FARMERS UNIONS

The smallest unit of the Farmers Union, the Farmers Union local, is similar to the subordinate Grange in that it is usually organized on a community or trading-area basis. In counties where there are several Farmers Union Locals, county organizations exist. These county organizations form the state organizations which now function in eighteen states.

Farmers Union locals also devote most of their attention to educational and social activities. The program of a local Farmers Union meeting, however, is likely to be heavily loaded with reports of the voting records of legislative and Congressional representatives, reports on local cooperatives and the business activities of Farmers Union affiliates, reports of young people's activities, discussion of the local health programs, analyses of proposals for farm-price supports, and of related social and economic reform measures. The educational and business meeting will be followed by a recreational program, as is also typical of local Farm Bureau and Grange meetings.

In states where the Farm Bureau organization is strong and Farm Bureau members work closely with the Extension Service, Farmers Union locals are likely to disagree with Extension educational programs in the economic field. In states such as North and South Dakota, where the Farmers Union is the dominant farm organization, relationships with the Extension Service are cordial and cooperative.

Farmers Union women are a participating part of the local, and do not have separate affiliated organizations as in the Farm Bureau and Grange. Most locals also have educational programs for Juniors (ages 14-21) and Junior Reserves (ages 6-14). Emphasis in these Junior programs is on farm and community problems. In several states young people who complete certain requirements of study and activity are awarded the initial payments on a life insurance policy in the Farmers Union Life Insurance Company. Farmers Union leaders oppose competitive activities in their youth programs.

Of the three farm organizations, the individual members and the local units of the Farmers Union give the most attention to national social and economic issues. They are not content to forward these resolutions to their county and state Farmers Union. The president or secretary of the local is usually authorized to forward them to the appropriate members of legislative bodies and administrative officers of programs related to the issues.

As in the case of the Farm Bureau and the Grange, the officers of the county units assist the locals in carrying out their programs. They also give counsel and direction to affiliated cooperatives, if any, and keep the state Farmers Union informed of their position on controversial issues. They perform this latter function primarily through the adoption of resolutions at one of their monthly meetings or at their annual meetings.

14

National Farm Organizations' Attitudes on Price Stabilization and Foreign Trade

In the last few chapters we have reviewed the development of national general farm organizations and the county and state activities of the three organizations, the American Farm Bureau, the National Grange, and the National Farmers Union. In this chapter we return to the farm problems discussed in Part I and analyze the current programs of these three farm organizations as they grapple with price stabilization and foreign trade. The position of the National Council of Farmer Cooperatives on these issues will also be indicated.

Preliminary to an examination of the ways in which each of these organizations attacks specific problems, a review of their more general beliefs will indicate the wide area of agreement among them on general objectives. The American Farm Bureau Federation, as a part of its guiding resolutions adopted for 1955, stated:

We believe:

That the present trend toward socialism, if unchecked, will lead to Communism. This is the greatest danger threatening our way of life.

In the American competitive system under which supply and demand in the marketplace are the ultimate determinants of price.

That every man is entitled to earn money honestly; to save, invest, or spend this money as he chooses; and to own any property he desires within the limits of the law.

In voluntary cooperation as a part of the American way of life.

That our economic system should be permitted to produce at the highest possible rate of efficiency.

That a person should be rewarded in accordance with his productive contribution to society.

That monopoly in any form is dangerous, whether it is by government, industry, labor, or agriculture.

That property rights cannot be taken away without jeopardizing the basic freedoms guaranteed by the Constitution.

That man's search for progress should be encouraged and should not be inhibited by false promises of security for all. . . .

The National Grange, in its booklet *Summary of Legislative Policies and Programs of the National Grange for 1955* states its agricultural objectives as follows:

During its 87 years of activity, one of the basic agricultural objectives of the Grange has been simple: to promote agricultural stability, prosperity, and progress. To achieve this objective in accordance with the traditions of American freedom and democracy, we have developed or supported policies which would provide these opportunities for farm families:

1. Opportunity to attain and retain farm ownership.

2. Opportunity for technological progress, through an adequate program of agricultural research.

3. Opportunity to obtain educational services in preparation for and the conduction of farm operations.

4. Opportunity to protect and strengthen the family farm ideal.

5. Opportunity to contribute to the efficient use and conservation of our soil, water, grass, timber, and wild life resources.

6. Opportunity to secure sound credit needed for the operation, expansion, and stabilization of farm operations.

7. Opportunity to maintain for themselves a level of income from investment, management, and labor comparable to that received in other segments of our economy.

8. Opportunity to operate their farms with a minimum of restriction or control by the Government.

The National Farmers Union, under the general heading, "Aims and Principles," in the opening paragraphs of its pamphlet *Farmers Union Program for 1954-55* is much less specific with respect to its general objectives. These opening paragraphs include the following:

The basic aims of National Farmers Union are based upon our understanding of the laws of nature and of God. Farming on the land we live close to nature. Our occupation depends on its life-renewing forces. Our livelihood requires its understanding. Our observation of nature's work gives us a thoughtful respect for living things and a profound regard for the essential dignity of the individual human being. We reaffirm our convictions of the truth and rightness of the ideals expressed in the Declaration of Independence and in the Constitution of the United States and its Bill of Rights. We are, therefore, opposed to the principles and practices of totalitarian dictatorship and shall continue to oppose the efforts of those who seek to impose on the people of this nation any type of economic or political dictatorship, whether in Communist, Fascist, or any other form. . . .

A review of the complete official statements of the three national farm organizations indicates that they are in accord with the views of the state leaders as they were described in earlier chapters.

At this particular stage in our history, the American Farm Bureau approaches specific farm problems from the general position that the individual should assume more responsibility to maintain his dignity, worth, and freedom and place less reliance on the national government; that recent emphasis on security should be shifted to more emphasis on individual freedom and responsibility; and that property rights should be preserved.

The National Grange, on the other hand, while holding most of these views, is more immediately concerned about the need for a continuing Federal farm program designed to bring farmers equality with other groups in income and living standards within a framework that is traditionally characteristic of a free people. The opening paragraphs of its official statement of legislative policies and programs for 1955 are devoted to an explanation of the need for a farm program related to the general agricultural objectives of the Grange quoted above.

The National Farmers Union, at this particular period in history, appears to be primarily concerned about equal rights and economic opportunities for all individuals, especially for the small farmers. In addition to the paragraph quoted earlier, the opening statements on aims and principles in *The Farmers Union Program for 1954-1955* include paragraphs asserting the right of each person to equality of educational opportunity, a belief that no person should be allowed to fall below an adequate standard of the necessities, conveniences, and comforts of life, and a conviction that each person, as the best judge of his own best interests, should have an equal voice in determining our laws. The statement on aims and principles includes several paragraphs on family farming and parity family living. Farmers Union members are sufficiently concerned about industrial-type agricultural enterprises to voice their objection to "the exploitation of human beings . . . whether on large individual or corporate owned factories-in-the-field or agricultural collectives imposed by totalitarian governments." They are convinced that farm families on family farms are a balancing force in our economy and "assert the right of farm families to be able to earn, by their own work, management, and property ownership, incomes equivalent to those earned by people in other occupations."

Price and Income Stabilization

Although all the farm organizations are concerned about the instability of farm prices and incomes, they differ in their proposed programs of action to achieve increased stability. The American Farm Bureau stresses the need for appropriate monetary and fiscal policies to maintain stable, high-level employment and economic activity in the economy as a whole. Farm Bureau leadership has been especially active in promoting such policies.

In addition to stressing the need for improved monetary and fiscal policies, however, the Farm Bureau resolutions for 1955 affirmed their support of "reasonable price protection through price support, production adjustment, and storage programs." Price-support and production-adjustment programs have a place in an over-all agricultural program, the American Farm Bureau asserts, because "we, as a Nation, sometimes fall short of achieving the more general policy objectives outlined above, and because of certain conditions peculiar to agriculture which cause farm prices to fluctuate more widely than farm costs."

The National Grange's program for achieving greater farm price and income stability includes expansion of markets through research, education, and sales promotion, expanded cooperative marketing programs, and multiple-price, self-financing measures for such commodities as can use them. The Grange recommends that legislation be provided whereby the producers of a given commodity such as cotton or wheat may be authorized to maintain a fair price for what is domestically consumed and to dispose of what may be surplus on world markets without depressing those markets.

The National Farmers Union favors policies and programs that its members believe will prevent farm income from falling below a level equivalent to 100 per cent of parity price on all family farm production. Toward this end, the Farmers Union urges the enactment of mandatory "100 per cent of parity" price supports on family farm production of all farm products. It specifically opposes the flexible price-support policy endorsed by the Farm Bureau and the multiple-price, domestic-parity program advocated by the Grange. The other farm organizations, on their part, oppose the mandatory price supports at 100 per cent of parity on all farm products which the Farmers Union favors.

With respect to the issues of equity involved in supporting the prices of some farm products and not those of others, the Farmers Union, as mentioned above, would extend mandatory price supports to all farm products. The Farm Bureau resolutions state:

Price support and production adjustment programs should take into account not only our experiences with existing programs, but also the differences that exist among commodities. For example, it must be recognized:

1. That some commodities are reasonably storable at moderate cost, while others can only be stored for short periods at a high cost or after expensive processing.

2. That some commodities are produced for sale, while others are produced primarily for use as livestock feed on farms.

3. That the shifting of acreage diverted from protected crops under government control programs creates serious problems. . . .

6. That producers are more favorably disposed toward production controls and price supports on some commodities than on others. . . .

The Grange resolutions do not deal specifically with this problem. They do, however, urge the "establishment and administration of Federal farm programs on a commodity by commodity basis," recognizing that there are "particular causes of inequity and depressed prices" in individual commodities that compel such an approach.

The National Council of Farmer Cooperatives does not mention price and income stabilization programs directly in its 1955 resolutions. It does, however, include the following statements with reference to the current cost-price squeeze in agriculture:

With constant increases in costs of production, distribution, and marketing, farmers have suffered losses in earning power and in economic stability to an extent which is cause for national concern.

Through maximum use of their own cooperatively owned, managed, and financed business organizations, farmers can make significant progress toward alleviating the present price-cost squeeze.

The value of such organizations in providing stability to our farm economy and furnishing farmers a means of establishing a greater stake in our free competitive enterprise system, while making a maximum contribution to the public interest, should be recognized and aided by governmental agencies and other segments of our economy.

CONFLICT BETWEEN SUPPORT PROGRAMS AND FOREIGN TRADE

While the Farm Bureau believes that in the long run variable price supports will ease the current conflict between domestic farm price-support programs and freer foreign trading policies, its resolutions do not propose any changes which would ease the conflict immediately. A long statement on international affairs includes the following:

The expansion of international trade on a mutually advantageous basis is of vital importance to the prosperity and security of the United States and cooperating nations. Our national welfare is so much affected by what happens in the international field that we cannot afford to deal piecemeal and on an unrelated basis with trade policies, foreign investments, technical assistance, and international defense measures. . . . Government should (1) establish a clear-cut, long-range policy on foreign economic relations and trade which includes the export and sale through private trade of the maximum quantities of farm products, and (2) consistently maintain that policy. . . .

U. S. farm products must be competitively priced to encourage vigorous merchandising by private traders. Full implementation of the Agricultural Act of 1954 will progressively improve the competitive position of U. S. farm products in foreign markets.

The Grange also devotes considerable space to foreign affairs. It affirms the importance of international trade in much the same terms as those used by the Farm Bureau. It states that it is the policy of the Grange to explore the possible use of a world food reserve into which surplus supplies can be placed and from which they can be withdrawn. The Grange supports "the principles of the Trade Agreements Act and the statutory escape clause procedure together with other Acts (Sections 22 and 32) for the protection of domestic agriculture and the extension of the Trade Agreements Act for a period of three years." In their advocacy of multiple-price, domestic-parity plans for export commodities they propose that these plans be safeguarded to prevent dumping, but look upon these measures as one way of expanding world trade.

The Grange in effect places economic protection of farmers ahead of freer international trade goals when they come into conflict. It defends the current practices of our government in the farm price-support field in the following paragraph:

We must make clear that any international agreement which does not make provision for the fundamental right of a given people to afford needed economic protection in the domestic market, and at the same time permit the products of that country to be actually competitive price-wise in the world markets, would be interpreted by us to be an invasion of the prerogative that is ours in our own domestic affairs.

In fostering this policy, however, the Grange maintains that industries which cannot meet foreign competition have no right to share in the expanding markets for their products as the nation grows.

The Farmers Union proposes to deal with any conflict between domestic-support programs and increased imports by preventing imports at prices less than 100 per cent of parity. Their statement on this subject follows:

Respecting imports of farm commodities that compete with domestic farm production, we favor adoption of policies that will give U. S. consumers an adequate supply at a fair price, preferably in connection with negotiated international commodity agreements, with provision for protecting 100 per cent parity returns to family farmers. If this can be done in no better way, we shall support an automatic flexible tariff that will eliminate imports at prices less than 100 per cent of parity.

In the international field the Farmers Union advocates the establishment of an international food and raw materials reserve supplemented by additional international commodity agreements similar to the International Wheat Agreement. It also advocates the fullest possible use of abundant U. S. farm supplies to further the aims of United States foreign policy.

The National Council of Farmer Cooperatives is concerned about achieving a freer international trade carried on by private industry. Its 1955 policy statements include the following on this subject:

Under the American system of free enterprise, private industry, rather than government, should occupy the position of primary importance in the field of foreign trade. This objective will require greatly expanded efforts on the part of farmer cooperatives and other segments of the economy. . . .

Various devices such as quotas, licenses, seasonal embargoes, bonus dollars, and many other restrictions have become of even greater significance in regulating and restricting international trade than [are] tariffs. . . .

The restoration of exports and international trade will come from increased economic strength in foreign countries, currency convertibility, the development of sound conditions which will tend to attract American capital abroad, and the elimination of many practices which hamper rather than encourage the exchange of commodities. We recommend these principles.

USE OF SURPLUSES TO RELIEVE WORLD HUNGER

There is substantial agreement among the farm organizations that our current farm surpluses should be used to feed the hungry peoples of the world to the extent practicable.

The Farmers Union urges donations of U. S. food to promote development of vocational training schools and other activities that will increase the productive ability of the country involved. It also urges the fullest possible use of the voluntary foreign relief organizations so that United States surpluses will actually reach the needy.

The Grange included a brief statement on the disposal of surpluses, urging that every effort be made to move surplus stocks of food to people who are in dire need through no fault of their own, both in this country and abroad. They also indicated their support of recently adopted Government policies which permit the sale of surpluses for foreign currencies and their barter for strategic materials essential to our national security.

The Farm Bureau maintains that most of our current farm surpluses can and should be bartered for goods desired by us or sold for foreign currencies which in turn may be used for our own purposes or loaned back to the importing country. The Farm Bureau resolutions state:

We believe that economic aid on a grant basis seldom accomplishes its intended purpose, but instead tends to weaken our economy as well as that of the recipient, and often diminishes U. S. prestige abroad. Except in disasters, we recommend that monetary grants be replaced by loans which assure the opportunity to repay the U. S. in goods or services. . . .

At another point the Farm Bureau resolutions state that a concerted effort is needed to get the facts concerning U. S. surplus agricultural commodities into proper focus for foreign buyers; that traders must be protected from actual or threatened give-away programs.

The 1955 policy statements of the National Council of Farmer Cooperatives do not deal with this issue.

BASIS FOR DIFFERENCES AMONG FARM ORGANIZATIONS

Differences among the farm organizations in recommended programs in this field are to be expected on the basis of the general background statements quoted earlier from their official programs or resolutions.

Implicit in the Farm Bureau resolutions is the belief that sufficient equity and justice and more freedom and more goods and services for everyone will result from greater reliance than at present on private trading in domestic and international markets. It is stated, however, that a substantial part of the domestic price-support, surplus-disposal, and marketing-agreement programs built up over the past twenty years should be kept. The Farm Bureau also believes that current farm price and income declines can best be met by a greater reliance on free markets than in the past. Its leaders are convinced that in the long run farmers will be benefited financially, and that the short-run losses in income will be amply repaid, by less governmental interference with farmers' decisions as producers, and more reliance on farmers' development of a better understanding of economics and greater skills in their vocation.

The National Grange resolutions and statements indicate a similar concern about the growth of governmental restrictions relating to domestic and foreign trade in recent years, but a greater concern than the Farm Bureau for the unfavorable consequences that might follow a return to freer market conditions. Specifically, they propose replacing existing price-stabilization programs with new ones worked out on a commodity-by-commodity basis with multiple-price programs similar to existing fluid-milk pricing arrangements put into effect where feasible.

The National Farmers Union, in contrast to the Farm Bureau, has little confidence in the equity and justice achieved by our market pricing system and less fear of excessive governmental regulation. It proposes mandatory price supports at 100 per cent of parity on all farm products and the removal of all production restrictions as quickly as possible. Any excess production would be distributed to low-income people in this country and sent to needy people in friendly countries.

In spite of these differences in general policy approaches, all three general farm organizations support a continuation of the existing payments to domestic cane and sugar-beet producers, and of import quotas, and also of controls on domestic sugar production. All three organizations also endorsed the new system of wool-price supports in the 1954 Agricultural Act, which sharply increased the level of supports to the domestic producers. Wool production in this country is only about one-third of domestic consumption. An enlarged direct subsidy to wool growers was supported, partly on the basis of equity, but largely on the basis of a belief that we should be more self-supporting in wool production in case of war.

All three general farm organizations also worked for the passage of the Agricultural Trade Development and Assistance Act of 1954 which authorized the President to use up to $300 million of surplus agricultural stocks for emergency grants to friendly foreign nations and in the sale of surplus farm stocks for foreign currencies over a three-year period. The Farm Bureau, however, opposed the inclusion of the authority for emergency grants up to $300 million.

In spite of individual leaders' differences, however, it is clear that the leaders in the Farm Bureau and the National Council of Farmer Cooperatives at the present time are reasonably well satisfied with the rules and regulations under which private trading is carried on; that the leaders of the Grange are less well satisfied; and that the leaders of the Farmers Union are distinctly dissatisfied. The word "socialism" has a radical connotation to the membership in all three organizations. Yet the changes in rules and regulations advocated by Farmers Union leadership are often attacked as "socialistic" by Farm Bureau leaders.

No doubt many factors have combined to bring about the differences in prevailing beliefs among farm leaders as to the best methods of achieving their common objectives. One of the important influences, however, must be the institutional history of the organizations. When the Farm Bureau was organized in 1919 it was concerned about the "radicalism" in organizations purporting to represent farm people. Their resolutions adopted in 1920 included the following statement on this topic:

We denounce radicalism in every form. We condemn the falsifier, the demagogue, and all who counsel, either by speech or writing, the over-throw of Amercan institutions.

We denounce any and all attempts on the part of the self-styled "Farmers' National Council" to ally the agriculturists of America with the radical element of the industrial world and we wish the American people to clearly understand that said organization has no authority to speak in behalf of farmers of this country.[1]

Throughout its history the Farm Bureau has maintained a similar position. Another differentiating factor may be the organizations' geographic origins.

The American Farm Bureau Federation finds its highest member-ship and its strongest and most persuasive leaders in the Corn Belt. Corn-Belt agriculture is probably the most diversified agriculture in the United States. Corn-Belt farmers are located reasonably close to the centers of population where their products are consumed, and livestock products produced on most Corn-Belt farms enjoy more stable prices than the grains and the fibers. The Corn Belt also enjoys a relatively stable climate with small fluctuations in acre yields from year to year.

One finds the greatest contrast if he turns next to the Farmers-Union leadership. The National Farmers Union was founded as a protest movement—a protest against the "inequity of farm incomes and the injustice of the low farm prices" when crop yields are favorable. Members of the Farmers Union tend to elect as officers individuals who have reputations as advocates of changes in existing rules and regulations governing private trading. The heaviest mem-bership in the Farmers Union and the ablest leaders are found in the Great Plains states where variations in weather and prices are much greater than in the Corn Belt. In North Dakota, one of the strongest Farmer-Union states, farm income from the sale of crops and livestock and livestock products increased sevenfold from the late 1930's to the late 1940s. Since the 1947-48 peak, North Dakota farmers' sales have dropped about 30 per cent even though costs have increased.

[1] American Farm Bureau Resolutions Nov. 14, 1919, and March 4, 1920.

Experiences such as these cause the more active leaders in the National Farmers Union to place major emphasis on price and income stabilization measures.

The National Grange has had a more varied institutional history than either of the other two general farm organizations. Starting out as a fraternal organization of farm people interested in the improvement of rural standards of living, it soon became a leader in the protest movements of the 1870s. In the last few decades, however, it has returned more nearly to its original objectives.

The intermediate position of the National Grange leadership at the present time is largely explained by the concentration of its membership in the Far West and in the Eastern states and by the greater interest of Grange leadership in fraternal activities and community service projects. Because of the wider range in interests and beliefs in the state leadership the actual policy statements adopted by the voting delegates in the National Grange are probably more of a compromise than those of either of the other two farm organizations. Support for multiple-price programs and for other changes in existing private trading regulations is greatest in the Western states and probably is acquiesced in by other Grange leaders in the interest of maintaining harmony within the national organization.

The leaders of the National Council of Farmer Cooperatives have had wide business experience and, as might be expected, devote most of their attention as officers of the Council to the problems cooperatives encounter in achieving maximum efficiency in marketing farm products and purchasing farm supplies. They believe that farmer cooperatives if widely supported and used by their membership can do a great deal to reduce the need for government action in price and income stabilization.

15

National Farm Organizations and the Problems of Low-Income Farmers and Hired Workers

As indicated earlier, the problems of low-income farmers and of the regular and migratory hired workers have received relatively little attention from national farm organizations. The American Farm Bureau Federation in its resolutions for 1955, deals with the low-income problem as follows:

Underemployed Rural People. There is a problem of rural underemployment which leads to low incomes and low living standards for some farm families even in a period of general prosperity.

Low incomes usually are a direct consequence of low production per worker. Underemployed families represent a large reservoir of untapped manpower that potentially could be much more productive either in agriculture or in industry, as well as a large market for the products of agriculture and industry. How well the advantages of education and training are made available to this group will affect the quality, competence, and attitudes of our future adult population.

We recognize the serious nature of this problem and urge a fuller use of the information and services made available through public education, the Cooperative Extension Service, and vocational training to assist in solving this problem. We recommend that State Farm Bureaus and the American Farm Bureau Federation give further consideration and study to this problem.

Farmers Home Administration. We favor continuation of direct government loans of the type handled by the Farmers Home Administration. As soon as a Farmers Home Administration borrower is capable of obtaining credit through other channels, provisions in the program designed to encourage him to do so should be adhered to.

We again urge that those in charge of administering the program avoid loans which encourage farmers to begin or continue uneconomic farming operations.

In its Summary of Legislative Policies and Programs for 1955, the National Grange endorses assistance to low-income farmers as follows:

Low Income Farmers. The National Grange believes that special attention must be given to ways and means of raising the income of farm families now receiving abnormally low incomes. In general, we believe improvement can be attained through a long-range, carefully planned effort to help low-income families (1) *increase their production of farm commodities or farm services, and/or* (2) *gain new income through non-farm employment.*

A primary goal, in seeking to increase production by those families staying on farms, should be the development of full-time, efficient, farm-family units of sufficient productive capacity to provide for equitable income and living standards. Also, credit in the amount and of the right type, assistance in total farm management, educational and research facilities, and technical help in expanding the size of the farm unit, should be readily available.

To assist in providing nonfarm employment for low-income rural families, cooperative studies with industries should be undertaken to determine present and prospective employment possibilities both in and away from the communities and both for part-time and full-time workers.

The National Farmers Union, in its program for 1954-55, recommends a program of action to solve the problems in this area as follows:

Programs for Low Income Farm Families. Immediate action should be taken to eliminate rural poverty and to solve the problems of low-income farm families. As many of these families as wish to remain in farming should be enabled to do so through assistance of federal and state programs to adjust their operations to sound economic family farm units. We support the following:

Farmers Home Administration. We are convinced that the great value of the Farmers Home Administration in developing adequate economic family farms is due to its unique service which combines adequate short, intermediate, and long-term credit with technical advisory assistance in a single package. We shall oppose all attempts to destroy this service by tearing its parts from each other. We urge greatly increased appropriations for Farmers Home Administration loans and technical advisory assistance to young farmers and other disadvantaged farm families to enable them to become established on fully adequate owner-operated family farms. As a supplement, we urge enactment of expanded conservation works and watershed protection programs, decentralization of urban industry, and vocational guidance and retraining programs. We shall continue to insist that the Farmers Home Administration and veteran-farm-loan programs be administered to retain the time-tested essential features of farm and home management technical assistance and that the authentic variable repayment plan be reinstituted.

The National Council of Farmer Cooperatives did not deal with the problems of low-income farmers, hired workers, or migratory workers in its 1955 policy statements.

REASONS FOR FARM ORGANIZATIONAL DIFFERENCES

The three general farm organizations differ somewhat in their proposals for dealing with the problems of low-income farmers, as might be expected from their varying historical development and different current beliefs. Again, a great deal of the difference can be explained in terms of the membership and leadership patterns of the organizations. The Farm Bureau was active in the 1940s in opposing the cooperative farming programs and a number of other activities of the Farm Security Administration on the grounds that they were unsound economic ventures, socialistic, and too costly to the taxpayer. Farm Bureau and other critics of the programs succeeded in getting a full-scale Congressional investigation of the agency in 1943-44. The American Farm Bureau was supported in a general way by the Grange, but the Farmers Union vigorously defended most of the Farm Security Administration's activities.

Some farm owners and operators who held leadership positions in the Farm Bureau looked upon many of the Farm Security Administration's activities as attempts to change the fundamental individual enterprise character of the rural American economy. Their attitude toward these activities of the Farm Security Administration was similar to the attitude of the Farm Bureau organizers toward "radicalism" in 1919-20. Their criticisms carried even greater weight in view of the poor management and economic failure of a number of the cooperative schemes. Congressional action supported the Farm Bureau position. In 1946 the Farm Security Administration was greatly limited powers.

Farmers Union support of the activities of the Farm Security Ad-
abolished and replaced by the Farmers Home Administration with
ministration, on the other hand, was in line with their historical

role as a protest organization. The Farm Security Administration was trying to help underprivileged rural people—people who were left at the bottom of the economic scale by the private enterprise economy. Farmers Union and several church groups fought valiantly to maintain a Federal agency with wide powers and substantial resources to assist low-income farm families. It is probable that popular support for the more restricted supervised credit programs of the Farm Security Administration was sufficient to assure their continuation.

However, the Farmers Union takes major credit for the passage of the Farmers Home Administration Act in 1946, which is the legislative authority for the current supervised credit program for low-income farmers. The Farmers Union has consistently lobbied for increased funds for these supervised credit programs. In contrast, although the Farm Bureau has supported the Farmers Home Administration, it has seldom if ever requested increased funds for the agency. Its leaders believed that if a high level of general business activity could be achieved and maintained this would go far toward solving the low-income problem.

NATURE OF RESPONSIBILITY IN THIS FIELD

Perhaps the first question to ask is whether farm organizations, made up primarily of family-type farmers, have a social responsibility with respect to the low-income rural groups described in Chapter 6. Then we need to ask ourselves: If the responsibility of organized groups is limited to their membership, who in our democracy should assume responsibility for the unorganized groups? In any event, largely because of the researches and public discussions of the low-income problem by agricultural economists, each of the three farm organizations indicated a concern for the low-income or underemployed farm families in their 1955 resolutions and legislative programs. This was the first time, however, that the low-income or underemployment problem in agriculture was mentioned specifically in the resolutions of the American Farm Bureau or the legislative program of the National Grange. The Farm Bureau in 1955 has gone even further and developed a discussion sheet to focus the attention of its members on the low-income farm problem.

This development, belated as it is, suggests that all leadership in farm organizations, representing largely commercial family farms, now recognizes a responsibility beyond the interests of most of their own members. One is impressed with the time lag which has existed between the discovery and analysis of a problem situation such as this and the development of a socially acceptable action program to correct it. At this writing the United States Department of Agriculture in cooperation with the individual states is starting pilot programs in approximately fifty counties in an attempt to develop a socially acceptable action program, although resettlement projects and Farm Security Administration activities were first undertaken twenty years ago.

Responsibility in the Area of Hired Workers' Problems

The American Farm Bureau in its resolution for 1955 had the following to say about hired labor:

Farm Labor. In many important farm production areas there continues to be a shortage of persons qualified and willing to perform certain types of farm work. This is particularly true during harvest and other seasonal peak periods.

A major source of farm workers to supplement available domestic workers is in our neighboring republic of Mexico.

We favor authorization for a continuing Mexican national farm labor importation program and reaffirm our support of the principles previously adopted relative to the features which should be incorporated in such program.

The British West Indies and Canada constitute other important sources of farm workers. We recommend continuation of present procedures for utilizing these and any other workers whose use may be authorized on our farms.

Present procedures relative to the employment of Puerto Rican workers in the continental United States are satisfactory and should be continued without material change.

We favor the complete independence of state employment services from federal control.

We are opposed to the licensing and regulation of farm labor contractors by the federal government. This is a function which may best be performed by state governments.

It may be noted that this resolution deals only with the interest of employers in adequate supplies of labor at all seasons of the year.

It is not concerned with the problems of minimizing seasonal variations in the use of hired labor or the treatment of hired workers and their families.

The National Grange limited its attention in the hired labor field to migrant labor problems. Its resolution on this subject follows:

Migrant Labor Problems. The National Grange recommends that in every community where there is a migrant labor problem, the entire community be urged to help the migrant laborer make the best possible social adjustment through the living, educational, social, and recreational facilities already available to him in the community.

The National Farmers Union includes a broad statement on labor relations in its *Farmers Union Program for 1954-1955.* This statement is as follows:

Labor Relations. We are convinced that the nation should establish conditions such that all the working people of the nation will be able to earn a fair share of national income. When the income of nonfarm people drops, the markets for farm products dry up; just as the demand for manufactured products falls when farm income drops. Therefore, we shall continue to support the enactment of public policies that will strengthen and protect collective bargaining and the right of workers to organize.

We recommend that the minimum wage law be expanded to cover all employees and that the minimum wage be raised to a figure consistent with current productivity and living costs. We shall support expansion of laws regulating safety, sanitation, and other working conditions to all places of work. We are convinced that the special federal aids given to industrial agricultural enterprises in the Alien and Migratory Worker Programs act to subsidize unfair competition against family farms; we therefore urge the elimination of these subsidies. All illegal immigration should be stopped. We wish to express our appreciation, as farmers, of the support given to farm programs by labor organizations."

The resolutions of the three farm organizations may suggest greater difference than actually exists in their attitudes toward hired and migratory labor.

State Farm Bureaus in some states such as New Jersey and Michigan have exercised leadership in improving the conditions under which migratory workers live and work, but the American Farm Bureau has never endorsed similar proposals for other states. This may be due in part to a belief that since most of the problems lie within the jurisdiction of the states (such as improvement in housing, health, and school facilities) resolutions in this field should be left to the state Farm Bureaus. However, as reported in Chapter 8, labor and church groups, the Farmers Union, and others convinced President Truman that the problems of migratory workers were sufficiently serious to justify the appointment of a special Presidential study commission in 1950.

The Grange is similar to the Farm Bureau in its concern with employers' problems. The Farmers Union position on the problems of hired workers including migratory workers, is only partially revealed by its statement on labor relations. While the majority of the members of all three farm organizations are family farmers, Farmers Union members are the only ones who, over a period of years, have passed resolutions critical of Federal farm labor programs. Those programs have been for the assistance of farm employers in getting hired workers when needed. Note the Farmers Union 1954-55 statement on this subject quoted above. In addition to their opposition to parts of Federal farm labor programs supported by special producer groups such as the sugar beet, vegetable, and fruit growers, and the other two general farm organizations, the Farmers Union joins with other welfare groups in support of the National Council on Agricultural Life and Labor. This Council is specifically concerned with problems of hired farm workers, migratory workers, and other rural families with low incomes and poor living conditions.

The interest of the Farm Bureau and of the Grange is to be expected. The particular type of hired-worker interest expressed by the Farmers Union is in part explained by its concern for protecting family farmers against the competition of large corporate, industrial-type farms. But Farmers Union membership has a long history of interest in the problems of both the hired-farm and nonfarm workers, which is probably explained by the belief of its leaders that through the years family farmers and industrial workers have many common economic interests.

While farm leaders are farm operators and many of them employ hired workers, at least occasionally, is it too much to expect farm organizations to concern themselves increasingly with hired workers' problems? The nature of farm leaders' social responsibility in this field appears to be similar to their responsibility in the support of rural churches, schools, and other community services. Yet they have less immediate interest in the special problems of their employees than in the community institutions in which their families participate. Perhaps in this area more than in any other, farm leaders responsive to a well-rounded code of ethics have opportunities and responsibilities to improve the conditions of rural life for individuals and groups having little bargaining power in our economic society.

16

National Farm Organizations and Land Tenure, Credit, and Soil Conservation Problems

The national farm organizations differ somewhat also in their programs relating to land tenure, credit, and soil conservation. All four organizations agree, however, on the goal of maintaining family farming as the dominant form of business organization in the agricultural industry. Also, all four of them have for years supported related activities which are necessary for a progressive system of family farming: comprehensive publicly financed research and extension programs, cooperative marketing, cooperative credit, and cooperative rural electrical associations.

Differences among the organizations show up in the specific policies and programs they support which have some, although not necessarily a direct, relation to the family-farming goal. A good example is the difference between the Farm Bureau and the Farmers Union regarding the importation of alien workers for employment largely by vegetable, fruit, and sugar beet producers. Since many of these producers are not family farmers, the Farmers Union opposes governmental programs of this type on the ground that competition with family farms is intensified by them. The Farm Bureau actively endorses such programs, since it believes many of the employers are family farmers and that alien workers are essential to the profitable operation of an important part of the agricultural industry.

The Farmers Union, in its literature and resolutions, suggests that there are powerful forces operating to supplant family farms by large-scale "factories in the field." It proposes, e.g., that price-support programs be limited to family farms.

The Farm Bureau and the Grange, on the other hand, do not look upon family farming as being in a precarious position and in need of special governmental assistance. They believe that family farms, because of their inherent strength, will continue in the current competitive situation to be the prevailing form of business organization in agriculture without special governmental assistance.

FARM ORGANIZATIONS AND LEASE IMPROVEMENTS

Students of land economics have made numerous studies of the effect of leasing practices on efficient farming methods, soil conservation, security of the tenant family, reduction in the year-to-year movements of tenants, and similar problems. Many land-grant colleges have developed educational programs based on these researches which are directed toward improvements in leasing practices. Farm organizations, however, have largely bypassed these problems.

There are a number of reasons for this. Legislative action in this field is reserved to the states under our system of government. It is probable that in states where lease-improvement problems have been more serious in earlier years state farm organizations have assumed an active leadership role. Evidence of their general inactivity is found, however, in the absence of legislation in most states embodying the general principles recommended by the land-grant college committee (see Chapter 9).

Only the Farmers Union included a resolution on leasing practices in its resolutions for 1955. It reads as follows:

We urge the adoption of state laws to provide security of tenure for farm tenants, including automatic renewal of leases, adequate notice of termination, compensation for unused value of improvements made by departing tenants, and minimum standards of housing and other improvements.

It seems probable that lack of action in this field is a reflection of the weakness of the political power of tenants as a group. While all three farm organizations accept tenants as well as farm owners as members, they also have many landlords within their membership. Attempts on the part of the interested tenants to get group action in this field result in divisions within the organization. Landlords usually are opposed to measures which strengthen the legal position of tenants. In the face of such division of interests the group pushes such problems aside and directs attention to problems common to a majority of its members.

While the problems of lease improvement are not as urgent as they were in the 1930s when farm tenancy was higher, they continue to be important. Much of the lack of more rapid progress in the adoption of soil conservation systems of farming in the Midwest and in the South can be laid at the door of outmoded leasing systems. The "run-down" appearance of many rented farms, of communities of rented farms, and of the schools and churches serving them, would gradually be improved if land tenure legislation in each state were brought in line with the recommendations mentioned earlier. It is in areas such as this that personal initiative is exercised by farm leaders. As an officer in a group where opposing interests are represented, must his role be limited to implementing the wishes of the majority? If he is personally convinced on the basis of ethical considerations and economic analysis that the demands of the minority for social action are in the general interest, what can he, as a responsible officer in the organization, do to assist them?

Farm leaders find themselves in this position more often than is generally supposed. Obviously, as a responsible officer of a group, a leader must obey the majority vote. The influence of a resourceful farm leader, however, makes itself felt in several ways. He may suggest ways and means by which the minority can improve the presentation of their case to the other members of the organization. He may personally help in overcoming misunderstandings and a lack of information among those members who have not been actively interested. As a result of such activities, in time the active minority group may win over a large number of members who are not directly affected by the proposed action. In this way a minority may achieve organization sponsorship of a measure which had been defeated by a majority vote months or years earlier. Such information and evidence as is available in the land-tenure field suggests that the need for improvements in this area should be a challenge to any farm leader who is concerned about his social responsibilities.

Farm Organizations and Credit

The Grange takes justifiable pride in the part it played in helping to bring the National Farm Loan system into existence in 1916. This occurred before the Farm Bureau had been organized and at a time when the Farmers Union was not active in national affairs. All three farm organizations supported the expansion of the cooperative Federal land-bank system, which made only farm real estate mortgage loans in the 1930s, into an expanded cooperative credit system. While the expanded Farm Credit Administration maintained the principle of cooperative organization in the new credit services, government capital and administrative assistance were furnished in its early years.

More recently the Grange, with the active assistance of the Farm Bureau, has taken the leadership in sponsoring legislation to make this cooperative credit system more independent of government as to both capital funds and administration. In spite of active opposition on the part of the Farmers Union, the Grange and the Farm Bureau secured the passage of legislation in the 83rd Congress which gave the cooperative farm-credit system an independent status, retaining only general supervision by the Secretary of Agriculture. The Farmers Union opposed this removal of the cooperative credit system from the Department of Agriculture because it believed that the government is more responsive to the credit needs of farmers, especially in adverse circumstances, than is an independent, privately-owned cooperative.

The position of the three general farm organizations on credit in recent years can best be shown by quotations from their latest resolutions on this subject.

In its official resolutions for 1955 the Farm Bureau states:

Adequate sources of credit at reasonable rates and on terms adapted to farmers' needs must be maintained. . . . The Farm Credit system has the purpose of providing sound and adequate credit facilities for farmers and farmer cooperatives at the lowest possible cost. We urge the adoption of methods and procedures . . . which will strengthen the cooperative features . . . and improve its services to farmers and farmer cooperatives. . . .

There is a definite need for longer-term production loans in many types of agriculture. To meet this need, we urge lenders to make production loans available for longer terms.

We believe that a credit program geared to the needs of young people who are not yet established in agriculture should be made more available. Present lending agencies should be able to supply these needs.

Note that the Farm Bureau does not ask for any expansion of government credit to meet the needs it has listed.

The Grange, in its Summary of Legislative Policies and Programs for 1955, limits itself to recommendations concerning the Farm Credit Administration and intermediate-length loans. Its resolutions on this topic read in part as follows:

It is our opinion that there is need for a kind of non-real-estate credit which will run for a period up to seven years. . . . Unless some contract can be devised which will assure farmers of renewal of short-term loans for periods up to seven years to ride out the ups and downs of prices and weather, we favor the establishing of loans with maturities up to seven years. . . .

The Farmers Union takes a somewhat different attitude toward the credit problem, as is indicated by the following statement on this subject in its program for 1954-55:

We assert the right of farm people to demand that the Federal government take an active role to make sure that there is ample provision for a plentiful supply of credit at a rate of interest no greater than required to cover cost of handling the money on terms adapted to all the needs of family farm operation, transfer of owner-ship, and development. We are opposed to national fiscal, monetary, and farm credit policies that lead to an increasing scarcity of credit and that permit and promote a rise of interest rates. We shall con-tinue to urge national policies that will reverse these adverse trends. . . . We shall work for establishment of a complete national farm credit system of private, cooperative, and governmental phases that will fully meet the needs of family farm agriculture.

FARM ORGANIZATION AND SOIL CONSERVATION

It was largely the enthusiasm, energy, and vision of Hugh Ben-nett, a soils specialist in the United States Department of Agricul-ture, and his associates, that resulted in the first modest soil-erosion research program in the late 1920s. This same enthusiasm, energy, and vision led to the authorization of a demonstration program of soil-erosion control under Bennett's leadership when the National Industrial Recovery Act was passed in 1933.

The early educational and propaganda activities of this new agency equaled or exceeded its demonstration activities. Conservation ac-quired a broad public appeal never before achieved in the history of this country. Within a few years most organized rural groups endorsed increased private and public efforts to conserve our soils, water, and other natural resources. The three national farm organizations at an early date shared in this endorsement of soil conservation activities.

In more recent years the farm organizations have differed in their support of specific soil conservation programs, largely because of differences in social philosophy and organizational structures.

The Farm Bureau, with its long record of support for the Extension Services of the land-grant colleges and its emphasis on the desirability of decentralization of governmental activities, for several years has favored decentralization of both the Soil Conservation Service and the Agricultural Conservation payments program. Its resolution on this subject for 1955 reads in part as follows:

The maintenance and improvement of our land resources through proper use is fundamental to any sound permanent farm program. This is of vital importance to the entire nation. The ultimate responsibility for wise land management rests with those who own or farm the land. . . .

Government has an important supplementary role in accomplishing wise use of land resources. The most important role of government is research, demonstration, and education. . . .

The national interest in wise use of our land and water resources justifies a measure of state and Federal expenditure for assistance to farmers for this purpose. The administration of such programs should be decentralized to the maximum feasible extent.

Appropriated funds for the Agricultural Conservation program should be allocated on the basis of conservation needs. Payments should not be made for practices which have become a normal and accepted part of farming operations in the area in which a farm is located.

In recent years the Farm Bureau has often favored smaller appropriations for the Federal Soil Conservation Service and the Agricultural Conservation Practice (payments) program than were recommended by the Appropriation Committees in Congress.

The Grange and the Farmers Union do not concur in the desirability of decentralizing the Soil Conservation programs. The key Grange resolutions on this topic for 1955 follow:

The Grange has long recognized the vital importance of wise use of natural resources, and has been a leader in helping to develop adequate soil and water conservation programs for American agriculture.

We recommend the attainment of a sound, adequate conservation program by:

1. The continuation of the Soil Conservation Service under the present financial and administrative form, with responsibility for carrying forward the programs developed by the locally administered Soil Conservation districts and for furnishing technical assistance in the development of small watershed conservation projects.

2. Appropriation of Federal funds for the Soil Conservation Service in sufficient amount to permit accelerated progress in the important work of protecting our vital soil and water resources. . . .

3. Providing adequate educational and technical assistance to farmers.

Comparable pronouncements by the Farmers Union urge that the agricultural conservation programs of the U. S. Department of Agriculture be maintained at levels equivalent to the social interest in preserving our farm land.

All three general farm organizations recognize the need for soil conservation activities and endorse government programs in this field. In terms of the issues raised when these problems were analyzed in Chapter 10, leaders in the farm organizations are agreed that farmers have not yet achieved land-use programs which conserve soil and water resources to the extent that is socially desirable. They are not agreed, however, on the most efficient methods of achieving the desired level of conservation on either privately or publicly owned lands.

Leaders in each of the three farm organizations might well ask themselves to what extent their position relative to the centralization or decentralization of a specific program is based on the efficiency in achieving agreed goals and to what extent it is based on other considerations. Even though questions are asked in this manner, it is doubtful that agreement could be reached on many aspects of the administration of the programs. Individuals with different backgrounds of training and experience and different ethical attitudes will continue to differ on such questions.

17

Farm Leadership in the Legislative Branch of Government

We turn now from an examination of the leadership activities in general farm organizations to a brief review of the opportunities and activities of farm leadership in legislative bodies. We include in the category of farm leadership the elected representatives of rural constituencies.

We would not, of course, expect to find elected representatives acting independently of their constituencies. Members of the legislative bodies in the states and in the national capital are elected to represent the people in their respective geographic areas. But they are more than errand boys for the folks back home. Each member of a legislative body may exercise a degree of leadership, while the leadership activities of chairmen of committees and subcommittees are quite substantial. As a background for appraising the farm leadership opportunities and responsibilities in this area it will be necessary to review the general nature of the legislative process.

KEY FUNCTIONS OF LEGISLATIVE BODIES

The functions of a legislative body are threefold: to formulate and pass legislation, to consult with or investigate executive agencies with a view to guiding legislation, and to inform the public. In each of these three fields, within the broad mandate received in the election process, each legislator may exercise independent initiative and judgment. Legislators in our democratic government have unique opportunities and responsibilities in practising social ethics and in shaping our economic life, for legislative bodies make many of the rules essential to the life of organized society. As pointed out in the opening chapter, most of our legislation from year to year deals with economic problems. As a result of the growth and development of the country, old rules and regulations become inequitable as between individuals and groups, or hinder efficient production and distribution. Also new needs, such as irrigation of farm lands in the non-arid sections of the United States, call for setting up rules and regulations where none existed before. The legislator's responsibility is to vote for those measures which will promote equity, productivity, and efficiency in economic life, with appropriate consideration for maintaining individual liberties and freedom in the broadest sense.

Exercise of Leadership in the Legislative Process

Legislative measures are likely to be controversial. Each legislator finds himself besieged by special-interest groups and by the more aggressive individuals in his district. Seldom does he get the same advice from all. On an issue on which his constituency is more or less evenly divided, the legislator has his greatest opportunity to exercise independent leadership. By taking the position which he believes to be in the general interest and informing his constituents of his reasons for doing so, a legislator may persuade a majority in his district to accept and support the position he has taken. There also is a great difference between merely voting for or against a proposal and working actively in committee meetings and in the legislative chamber to secure adoption or defeat of a particular measure.

The conscientious legislator must form a thoughtful judgment on all the issues on which he is called to take action. In actual practice most legislators become specialists in one or more fields and outside the fields of their specialty accept the judgment and leadership of others in whom they have learned to have confidence.

Most elected representatives have much the same beliefs as the majority of the electorate in their districts. Their own judgment of how the general interest bears upon a specific issue usually coincides with the majority of the voters in their districts. A good example of this is found in the views of Congressmen on the free trade issue. Senators and Congressmen from "protectionist" districts usually believe sincerely that protective tariffs are desirable not only for their respective districts, but also for the entire country. The converse holds true for representatives from districts which would benefit from freer trade. There are situations, however, when the legislator (usually because he is more fully informed on the subject) personally believes in the desirability of a specific legislative action although a majority of the people he represents believe the opposite. Some legislators faced with this dilemma vote "their convictions"; others conform to the opinion in their districts. Well-informed and able legislators have expressed their real convictions by opposing measures in committee meetings but have voted otherwise on roll call in the legislative chamber. No final answer can be prescribed for all such situations. It is in the variants of this situation that one finds many of the opportunities for leadership in the legislative branch of government.

Soon after he arrives at the state or national capital, the elected representative finds that some facts relative to the situations he discussed with the voters at election time have changed. He himself may acquire a fuller understanding of the issues involved during the debates in the legislative chamber. What is the legislator's responsibility when he acquires new information and understanding not possessed by the voters in his district? If there is time before legislative action is required, a common practice is to give this new information to the voters back home by reports disseminated through local news agencies. Legislators exercise significant leadership in this way.

An even more widespread—and a subtle—method of exercising leadership is inherent in the legislative process. A typical situation is one where the electorate has little information on the specific issue under consideration. The elected representative weighs the information available to him and takes a position. Sometime later, at the latest during the next election campaign, he explains to the voters why he believes the position he took was the correct one. It is most important that the individual legislator make the decision which is right; i.e., the decision which correctly evaluates the ethical and economic issues involved and contributes to the general welfare. A sound decision, followed by a vigorous explanation of the reasons for taking this position, is the means by which progress is made in a democratic society. Conversely, one weakness of our democracy is the possibility that a legislator may take a position to please a few important special interests in his district, yet make the voters believe that he has acted in their interests. Many of our social and economic issues are so complex that it is all too easy to mislead the lay public for a considerable period.

THE IMPACT OF PRESSURE GROUPS

In agriculture, as in every other field, a large number of special interests may be affected by each new legislative action. In addition to the special producer groups such as the wool growers, the poultrymen, the dairy producers, and the citrus fruit growers, marketing organizations and such firms as those which produce fertilizer, insecticides, farm machinery, and processing equipment are organized into trade associations and have representatives in many state capitals and in Washington. A member of the Senate or the House of Representatives in the national government gets conflicting counsel from many of these special producer and trade groups. In some instances he gets conflicting counsel from the general farm organizations. Most legislators become familiar with the needs of special interests, but rely most heavily on the attitudes found in their home districts. Legislators, as might be expected, are particularly interested in the recommendations of their own local units of the national farm organizations. They keep in touch with the voters' interests through the editorials, news items, and letters published in the local newspapers, by frequent visits back home, and by special polls.

Legislators in the national capital in particular recognize that there is a difference, sometimes large and sometimes small, between the views of the national officers of an organization and the views of its rank-and-file members in a particular geographic area. They tend to discount the views of the national leaders unless evidence indicates that the home folks really do hold these views. For this reason it is most important for the officers of a "pressure group" to maintain close contact with its members and secure the support of a united membership. A legislator is more interested in the views of the membership in his district than in the views of the national leaders. He may not have full confidence in the ability of even the state officers to speak for the membership because of the wide gap between officers and members in some organizations. A frequent comment of legislators is that they can't take action as recommended by the national officers of an organization because "they haven't yet sold it to their members and to the other interested groups."

IMPORTANCE OF APPROPRIATIONS COMMITTEES

Members of the appropriation committees in the state legislatures and in the National Congress exercise great influence in the rural welfare field. Their official responsibility is to recommend the appropriations needed for administering state and Federal laws.

"Control of the purse strings" has always been important. It has increased in importance in recent years as a result of the additional regulations, services, and educational programs undertaken by the state and national governments. The budget of the United States Department of Agriculture now includes around $100 million each for the Agriculture Research Service, the Agricultural Marketing Service, and the Commodity Stabilization Service. The Agricultural Conservation Program Service, which makes direct payments to farmers for the performance of soil conservation practices, has disbursed in recent years $175 to $225 million. Loan authorizations to the Rural Electrification Administration and the Farmers Home Administration have exceeded $350 million annually.

Legislators play a strategic leadership role in their appropriation activities. They have it within their power to increase or decrease the financial support for specific regulations, services, and educational programs. Well informed, ethically sensitive legislators, utilizing the techniques now available to them for informing the public regarding appropriation issues and obtaining guidance and counsel from interested groups, can do much to promote rural welfare through their activities on appropriation committees.

LEADERSHIP RESPONSIBILITIES IN UTILIZING INVESTIGATIVE POWERS

The importance of the investigative function of legislative bodies has been increasing in recent years as our social and economic life becomes more complex. This function also appears to be most susceptible to abuse.

Legislators exercise a key leadership role in three aspects of the investigation process. First, they determine whether or not to authorize an investigation. This decision takes the form of determining which applications for funds for special investigations should be approved. All standing committees of Congress have investigative powers, but investigations requiring more funds than are authorized for the standing committees require special appropriations.

Legislators who are members of special investigating committees or subcommittees exercise leadership, second, in determining the character of the investigation. Because of the special interests involved in every case, the responsible legislator must be active in making sure that, as the investigation goes forward, it is conducted in an impartial manner and with appropriate regard for the rights of the individuals and institutions involved. The third responsibility of a legislator is to assist in getting such legislative action as is needed to correct inequities or abuses uncovered by the investigation. A number of important legislative measures, such as the bill setting up the Farmers Home Administration in 1946, have been drafted at the close of a special investigation.

Special Responsibilities of "Farm" Representatives

Elected representatives from predominantly farm districts have the same general leadership opportunities and responsibilities as elected representatives from other districts. In a sense, each legislator has the same opportunities and responsibilities except for differences which may arise out of offices held in the legislative body. From another point of view, however, legislators from predominantly farm districts have special opportunities and responsibilities that grow out of the nature of the farm problems.

One of the key questions with which they are faced is whether or not farmers are disadvantaged by the economic power exercised by other groups in our modern industrial society, and hence need special governmental price- and income-stabilization programs. The three general farm organizations agree on this issue, but differ on the nature of the programs that are desirable. The legislator from a farm district has a responsibility to examine the reasons behind the differences among the farm organizations on this point. He can assist in working out compromises when farm groups fail to agree. Where the groups represented in his constituency fail to agree, as is often the case, he must arrive at an independent decision if he is to discharge his responsibilities not only as an elected representative from a farm district but as an integral part of a government concerned with the welfare of all the people in the country.

Another aspect of the farm problem, closely associated with the instability of farmers' prices and incomes, is the tendency of farm production to outrun available markets in peacetime. This may not be a permanent aspect of the farm problem, but it was present in the 1920s and gives every evidence of being of major importance in the years immediately ahead. Legislators from farm districts have a special responsibility in this area. Publicly financed research and education programs have been largely responsible for the rapid increases in farm output in the past decade. Will our public investment in agricultural research produce new discoveries that result in increasing farm production faster than market outlets become available? If so, should we turn to restrictionist practices, or should we assist private enterprise in expanding market outlets more rapidly? Have we developed such a large group of production-minded scientists that our public investment in research and education is oriented too much toward efforts to increase immediate production and too little toward achieving more efficient distribution, wider markets, and a better balance between income-earning opportunities in farming and in other occupations?

Legislators from farm districts, as distinct from the officers or leaders in organized farm groups, represent all the people in their districts. Probably about half the families in rural areas are not members of any of the general farm organizations. In a democracy such as ours it is highly important that we have ethically sensitive representatives who familiarize themselves with the problems and the needs of the unorganized and often disadvantaged individuals in their districts. While the record is not too good in this respect, improvement is being made. Further progress in the solution of the problems of tenants, low-income farm families, regular hired workers, and the migratory agricultural workers rests to a great extent on the actions of informed, ethically sensitive, elected representatives, Federal and state, from districts where these people live in substantial numbers.

18

Farm Leadership in the Executive Branch of Government

On first consideration there appears to be a conflict between the role of an able impartial administrator in the executive branch of government and the exercise of farm leadership. However, this chapter will indicate the farm leadership opportunities that do exist in the executive agencies and describe some of the techniques successfully used in discharging the leadership responsibilities inherent in administration.

In contrast to the functions of the legislative branch of the federal government already outlined, the executive branch is charged with administering existing legislation and recommending changes in or additions to existing legislation. Officers of the executive branch have leadership opportunities and responsibilities in carrying out both of these functions. Moreover, these opportunities and responsibilities are shared by all policy-making individuals in the Department of Agriculture. They are shared also by policy-making officials in other departments which deal with such farm problems as the importation of foreign workers, foreign trade, and maintenance of pure food standards.

STATEWIDE AND NATIONAL CHARACTER OF EXECUTIVE LEADERSHIP

The Secretary of Agriculture or a state commissioner of agriculture looks at farm problems in a different focus from that of the elected representative. The Secretary, for example, must view any particular problem from the standpoint of the entire country and the entire industry. In contrast, the legislator characteristically tends to view a problem first from the standpoint of his own district, and only secondarily from a national viewpoint. A Secretary of Agriculture also must harmonize his agricultural leadership activities with the general position of other members of the Cabinet and with the position of the President. He cannot, for example, further such foreign-trade policies involving farm products as are inconsistent with the policies of the President and the Department of State. In recent years an increasing number of farm issues affect several departments of the national government. The departments of government, all being equal, cannot readily resolve issues on which there is basic disagreement. Such issues may be referred to the White House Staff for resolution. Although the commodity groups, the marketing organizations, and the general farm organizations are often consulted by the White House Staff, at this stage greatest weight is given to the national interest in contrast to the strictly agricultural interest.

Within the above limitations, the Secretary of Agriculture, the Under Secretary, and the assistant secretaries are the most influential farm leaders in the United States. They have a large and competent staff. They have an extensive information service. And they have wide latitude in the interpretation and administration of farm legislation.

Leadership Opportunities in Administration

As a general rule, legislation is worded in sufficiently broad terminology to require the administrators to face equity and economic issues essentially similar to those faced by the legislators in deciding on the specific wording of the legislation. The administrators of a soil conservation program, e.g., must decide, within the broad limits of the enabling legislation, how to allocate the funds and personnel among the states and local soil conservation districts, and how to balance the work programs, as for example between individual farm planning, technical assistance in agronomic practices, and technical assistance in engineering practices. They also may give assistance on a "first come, first served" basis, in which case most of their services will be utilized by the larger and more progressive farmers; or they may develop a better-balanced program by building up interest among the smaller and less progressive farmers. The drafting of each administrative directive and regulation involves ethical and economic issues.

INTEREST GROUP INFLUENCE IN ADMINISTRATION

One of the best indications of the wide latitude for leadership in administration is the great amount of time and effort spent by interest groups in influencing administrative decisions. National marketing organizations and other groups, such as the National Wool Growers Association, the Sugar Beet Producers Association, the National Milk Producers Federation, the Association of Soil Conservation Districts, the National Council of Farmer Cooperatives, and the general farm organizations, spend as much or more time and effort on educational work and counseling with their members relative to administrative decisions than they spend on legislative issues. They also spend as much or more time counseling with administrators in the Department of Agriculture than in influencing the members of the legislative branch of government.

An able and resourceful officer in an interest group who has been canvassing his membership relative to alternative administrative decisions transfers his attention to the administrative agency immediately after the passage of enabling legislation. In earlier days interested industries often were successful in getting some of their spokesmen appointed to administrative positions. This still happens occasionally; but the more common practice is to try to make sure that unfriendly administrators are *not* appointed. General farm organizations and the specific industry affected are often consulted by the government for their views regarding the qualifications of candidates for a key administrative position.

Unfortunately, the organizational forces in trade and industry groups operate somewhat in a vicious circle so far as influence on administrative actions is concerned. A group organizes to achieve a measure of political and economic power for its members and to correct what is regarded as an inequitable situation which has developed. It employs a paid staff and is successful in achieving the immediate objective. But the paid staff or salaried officers must continue to "show results" year after year in order to justify a continuation of their jobs, salaries, and expense accounts.

First they convince the members that a specific administrative decision is desirable; then they "persuade" the administrator. And finally they report to the membership that through their efforts the members' interests have been protected, and the "correct" administrative decision has been made.

Obviously the administrator should be fully as sensitive to the ethical issues involved in his administrative program as are the members of the legislative branch which enacts the legislation. Good administration involves far more than accurate appraisal of the strength of opposing interest groups. It involves obtaining a clear understanding of the ethical and economic issues in alternative administrative decisions within the authorization of the legislation. It requires decisions and administrative actions that result in a minimum of inequity, and also a minimum of interference with economic forces which promote efficiency and productivity; or, conversely, it requires actions which increase equity, efficiency, and productivity.

The good administrator seeks to create situations which permit him to make the right decisions. He learns to utilize the staff and officers of the interest groups with which he works, so as to achieve the end he desires—fair and efficient administration of the program authorized by the legislative body.

By ascertaining their organizational biases in advance it is often possible to let the staff of an interest group take credit for certain administrative decisions or changes, thus winning their cooperation and diverting their attention from other activities which could not be permitted by an administrator concerned with promoting the general welfare. Here it is not always easy to draw a line between legitimate strategy and "playing politics."

LEADERSHIP IN RECOMMENDING LEGISLATIVE CHANGES

Experienced administrators agree that there is more opportunity for achieving increased welfare (more equity and increased productivity) through better administration of existing legislation than through changes. Yet legislative changes are needed from year to year, and administrators have a great opportunity and responsibility in relation to the changes they recommend.

The unique position of an administrative agency in making legislative recommendations is well illustrated in the development of the Agricultural Act of 1948. All interested agricultural groups were agreed that new legislation was needed after the expiration of the wartime price supports on December 31, 1948. Each of the general farm organizations had the guidance of resolutions passed by its delegate bodies, but found it difficult if not impossible to draft a specific, comprehensive legislative proposal. The technical staffs of these organizations are small in comparison with the technical staff in the Department of Agriculture. So also are the staffs of the legislative committees of the Congress which deal with agriculture.

For these reasons the Secretary of Agriculture was asked to make recommendations for new legislation. Following the presentation of working-committee reports and more specific suggestions by the Secretary of Agriculture, the Solicitor's office of the Department of Agriculture was asked to draft specific legislative bills in consultation with the chairmen and staffs of the legislative committees.

Organized interest groups then had concrete proposals to consider. They endorsed the major features of the departmental draft but made suggestions for modification at certain points in line with their guiding resolutions. Different segments of the agricultural industry and the three general farm organizations made different recommendations on a number of points, but all endorsed the major features of the departmental draft. It remained for the legislative committees and the members of the House and Senate to reconcile the conflicting recommendations on specific points and arrive at a workable compromise. The administrative staff of the Department of Agriculture was relied on for expert testimony and exercised a decisive influence in determining the general character of the Agricultural Act of 1948.

The administrative staff will always exercise a key role in proposing additional legislation, for they have the intimate knowledge and experience growing out of administering the enabling acts adopted by the legislative branch. Legislators must go to them for a report on the accomplishments of the legislation enacted earlier.

But the advice and counsel given the legislative branch will depend almost as much on the ethical and economic views of the administrator as on his administrative experience. Without ethical sensitiveness and an accurate economic analysis of social and economic problems, an otherwise successful administrator may be blind to the indirect effects of a certain piece of legislation. Social scientists on many occasions have lamented the "short-sighted" views of administrators of complex social and economic legislation. The leadership opportunities and responsibilities of the administrator in relation to legislative recommendations are probably greater than those of any other individuals in our society.

THE EXECUTIVE BRANCH AND UNORGANIZED GROUPS

Special organized groups "protect" the interests of the producers of special products, and the general farm organizations represent the commercial farm families. Although the general farm organizations give some attention to the problems of low-income farmers, tenants, and beginning farmers, they give less attention to these groups than do the social scientists. Both the legislative and the executive branch of government are kept aware of the problems of the middle-income and large-scale farmers. The problems of the low-income farmers, the small farmers, the tenants, and the beginning farmers, however, seldom get the attention they deserve in any comprehensive examination of the efficiency, productivity, and equity problems of our rural economy.

Leaders in the executive branch of government have an opportunity to redress this imbalance somewhat. By the studies they authorize and by the publicity given to the results of studies in this area, they can do much to make other groups in society aware of the situations that exist.

At the risk of repetition, this can be illustrated by the current interest in the problems of low-income farmers. Their problems have been analyzed for twenty years by the social scientists in the Department of Agriculture, the land-grant colleges, and the privately endowed universities. Largely as a result of the information made available by these continuing studies, all three farm organizations have adopted resolutions on this problem; President Eisenhower in 1955 sent a special message to Congress recommending that a pilot remedial program be undertaken in fifty counties where the problems are most acute, and this project has been started. Several Senators and Representatives for the first time introduced bills on the subject in the 84th Congress (1955). While at this writing it is too early to anticipate additional administrative and legislative actions, it is evident that more progress can be expected in this neglected field.

Administrators in the executive branch of government have the same responsibility with respect to unorganized groups and individuals as have the elected representatives in the legislative branch. The Chief Executive is elected by popular vote of all the people. He and his staff are responsible for administering the laws in the interest of all the citizens. While this is generally understood, in our highly organized society it is easy to become occupied with the problems of the organized groups and to forget substantially unorganized groups in rural areas whose interests are not fully represented by the well-known general farm organizations and industrial associations.

19

Concluding Observations

This chapter attempts to summarize and recapitulate the most important situations and problems treated in Part I, with accompanying references to the related attitudes and activities of farm leaders and organizations discussed in Part II, and with further comment on the ethical issues involved.

Group Interest and General Interest

In Chapter 1, the relation of ethics to economic philosophy and legislation was discussed on the assumption that equity (defined as "fairness" or "evenhanded impartiality") is a basic ethical goal in our society, largely shaping the legislation and other rules governing economic life.

Farmers, like other economic groups, organize to reach goals that they cannot attain by individual action. These goals often conflict with the interests of certain other individuals and groups—or with more general interests shared by many or all groups. Public policies worked out over the years reflect compromises between these conflicting interests, necessary adjustments and readjustments to changing conditions, and pursuit of the goal of equity as an underlying and balancing influence.

Farm leaders demonstrate the quality of their leadership in their contribution to equitable solutions of farm problems. They assist members of their respective groups both in formulating goals and in attaining them. In a democratic organization effective leadership involves a two-way operation. Participation of membership at all levels in considering group problems and interests requires an active information service and a continuing educational program. Thus leaders have opportunity to advise and to be advised, so that policies adopted may be as far as possible an achievement of the entire organization.

Farm leadership at its best tries to keep farm groups aware of the relation of their problems, policies, and goals to the interest of society as a whole. For a democratic society will not long respect the claims of a merely self-seeking group. A leader needs not only skill in adjusting disputes within his own organization and in negotiating with other groups but also statesmanship that sees the interests of his group in the setting of the general interest.

Special Needs of Agriculture

Some farm leaders maintain that agriculture has so fundamental a place in our economy that its problems and needs deserve priority in public policy. This attitude is perhaps an inheritance from the time when a majority of the people of the United States were engaged in agriculture, and when farm production made up the greater part of the economic output. Manufacturing was mainly an accessory to farming. Most of the fiber produced here, for example, was shipped abroad for manufacture. Transportation by canal and then by rail was developed mainly to meet farmers' needs. Mining began to be important only in the 1850s. More than anything else, agriculture was the nation's business for most of the nineteenth century.

It is still a basic industry, of course, though it now employs not more than 10 per cent of the gainfully employed, and though its production as shipped from the farm constitutes now only a minor fraction (less than 6 per cent) of the gross national product.

Government aid has been needed not only because of the importance of agriculture as a basic industry but also because of notable differences between agriculture and other industries.

The ownership of farm land and of tools of farm production is so widespread that falling prices of farm products create a far-reaching credit problem throughout the nation. In no other industry is ownership so widely distributed.

The biological nature of agricultural production makes its response to economic forces slow. There can be no quick adjustment of production to variations in the market. Nor can farm labor—furnished mostly by a family—be shifted to other employment or secure unemployment compensation. A business recession normally affects farm prices most seriously and for the longest period, involving insofar as possible a large-scale readjustment of the use of resources.

As a result of public and private research and educational programs, the rate of technological progress and hence the increase of farm output tends in peacetime to exceed the rate of market expansion. This has been true during the past thirty-five years, and promises to continue for the foreseeable future even though population is increasing rapidly and international trade may become freer. The effect is a burdensome supply of farm production, falling farm prices, and decline in real farm income—while other economic groups may be doing well.

Also, there are more than a million farms where for some years families have earned incomes of less than $1000 a year from all sources. This is largely because their farms are too small and unproductive and their communities offer no other employment opportunities. Throughout the war and our most prosperous years of peace, these low-income farms have contributed only children to our economy, and have received little from it.

Measurement of the economic welfare of farm groups as compared with other economic groups is a difficult undertaking. Per capita income statistics are often used to show that farm people are only about one-half as well off as nonfarm people. But this comparison lumps together farmers living on productive and unproductive farms, and on residential as well as commercial farms; it discounts rental value of farm housing, food, and fuel, and ignores comparative size of rural and urban families. However, the data for nonfarm people are similarly questionable for such a comparison. Yet there is a fairly clear indication of substantial disparity of income between otherwise comparable farm families and urban families—the most serious discrepancies being between full-time farm families producing little for commercial markets and families of employed skilled and unskilled urban workers.

Parity price ratios are used even more widely to measure the relative economic position of farmers. In some chosen base period, such as 1910-14, the price of a certain farm product (say 100 bushels of wheat) is compared with what it would buy in goods used by farmers in production and family living (also interest and taxes) today. If that is the parity price, then variations at other times in what 100 bushels of wheat will buy of the other goods will indicate whether the price of wheat is above or below parity. The computation is not so simple as stated, but that is the principle of the operation. It is accepted for legislative and administrative purposes as an approximate measure of equity; but it does not provide conclusive proof that farm families are either better off or worse off in comparison with other economic groups than they were in 1910-14.

The search for formulas by which the special needs of agriculture may be equitably measured and met will doubtless go on. The relative positions of groups change from time to time, as do their special needs. Farm leadership has a responsibility to keep informed as to the need for corrective action and the social and economic conditions affecting the situation.

PRICE AND INCOME STABILIZATION

In recognition of the special needs of agriculture, the government has undertaken various programs for stabilizing the prices of farm products—to prevent them from fluctuating as widely as under free market conditions. It was noted above that farm economy is not readily adjustable to wide market changes. Therefore farm income is protected to a certain extent.

Three types of price-stabilization programs are now in operation: (1) a mandatory price-support program for six basic and five nonbasic commodities, the means being government loans and purchases; (2) support of prices of other farm products up to 90 per cent of parity at the discretion of the Secretary of Agriculture, using similar means; (3) marketing agreements and orders to regulate the marketing of specified fruits and vegetables in certain areas and the marketing of fluid milk in about fifty urban markets—these agreements and orders having been approved by the producers supplying the respective markets.

Farm leaders disagree on some aspects of these programs. The Farm Bureau favors lower and more flexible price supports than do the National Grange and the National Farmers Union, and does not favor extending price supports to additional products. The Farmers Union favors 100 per cent of parity. The National Grange would treat each commodity separately, and apply a multiple-price domestic parity program[1] to export crops.

[1] See pages 100-101.

THE DISPOSITION OF SURPLUSES

It has been often suggested that price supports be kept at relatively high levels, maximum protection be maintained, and accumulated surpluses be used to feed and clothe the needy in friendly foreign countries. Economists regard such a policy (except perhaps in an emergency) as self-defeating. We should be failing to use resources for some other economic need, and at the same time not creating conditions favorable to self-help abroad. Our current surpluses should be used as far as possible to finance economic expansion programs in underdeveloped countries; our technical aid programs are so far only a start on a large and fruitful undertaking.

The farm organizations seem to be in substantial agreement on this issue, though the National Grange and the Farmers Union go further than the Farm Bureau in favoring public donations and distribution of existing surpluses through private charitable organizations.

THE LOW-INCOME FARM FAMILIES

Farm leaders have an unusual challenge in the low-income farm problem. It has persisted in spite of wartime demands for all-out production of both farm and nonfarm products and through our most prosperous peaceful years. Although these low-income farms are almost as numerous as the larger, more productive family farms which produce over 85 per cent of the farm products marketed, farm programs of the past twenty-five years have been of very little assistance to them.

The United States Department of Agriculture, in cooperation with the states where these low-income farm families are most numerous, has started a series of pilot remedial programs in approximately fifty counties. These programs include special educational and credit facilities, improved labor-placement services, and vocational training programs.

Whatever the right solution of the problem, the gravity of it is at last receiving more attention.

Thus far, however, the general farm organizations made up of family farmers have given relatively little special attention to this persistent problem. The Farmers Union has been most active, particularly in working for an expanded supervised credit program for these families. Social scientists in their persistent study and educational activity in relation to these problems have had a large part in making both the general public and the farm leaders aware of the special problems of low-income farm families.

All three general farm organizations in their policy statements for 1955 indicated that they are now concerned about these problems and will support programs for dealing with them in the future. Since the farm organizations are primarily concerned with the interests of their members, however, the ethically sensitive farm leaders have the special responsibility of keeping the members informed of and interested in the solution of these problems, which have been regarded as outside of their ordinary concern.

HIRED FARM WORKERS

Farms are not operated by owners or tenants alone. About two million people who are neither owners nor tenants work on farms for wages as their regular or part-time occupation. We hear or read comparatively little about them in discussions of farm problems.

The distinct groups are the "regular" hired workers and the migratory workers. The rest are casual nonmigratory workers, such as men and women who work intermittently on different farms in their community and otherwise may be self-employed or engaged in non-farm work. The casual workers may outnumber either of the other groups, but are not easily classified. It is the situation and problems of the "regular" hired workers and the migratory workers that are beginning rather tardily to receive attention.

The "regular" hired workers, who work continuously on one farm most or all of the year, make up about a third of the 2 million mentioned. In 1953, 63 per cent of them were married. The average annual wage was about $1200 in cash plus house rental and farm produce (or board and room for the unmarried). All comparisons indicate that farm wages are near the bottom of the wage scale. In these circumstances many farmers have had to increase wages and improve housing in order to meet the competition of nonfarm employers; but low prices for farm products, out-of-date management practices, and inadequate land and facilities rather than deliberate exploitation account for the continuing low wages and poor living conditions of most hired farm workers. Minimum standards have been set up in some states designed to relieve some of the worst conditions, but farm organizations have given the situation little attention.

The number of domestic migratory workers including working children under 14 was estimated at 450,000 in 1952, but in addition a large number of Mexicans came into the country as usual for temporary farm work. These family groups that travel together for seasonal work serve a useful purpose especially in fruit and truck-crop sections where many workers are needed at certain times but not for the rest of the year. Little attention has been given until recently to the social and economic problems involved in this type of employment. Apparently church and community organizations must take the lead in pressing for legislation dealing with these problems, especially as to housing, health, and school attendance of children.

LAND TENURE AND FARM CREDIT

Farm leaders have given much less attention to needed tenure and credit improvements in the last two decades than the relative importance of these problems warrants. Tenure and credit practices in the rural communities are responsible for the progress or lack of progress made in solving many other problems: soil conservation, school and church improvements, adoption of improved farm practices, and community recreation projects. They also are an important factor in determining which of the young people stay in the community and which migrate to other communities.

All farm organizations have supported the expansion and strengthening of the cooperative farm credit system. At the present time the three general farm organizations urge banks and cooperative credit institutions to make amortized loans extending over a period of several years to finance machinery and livestock purchases and farm improvements.

Land-tenure legislation falls within the jurisdiction of the states. The Farmers Union is the only national farm organization that mentioned land-tenure problems in its 1955 policy statements. Very few of the states have tenure legislation which adequately protects the tenant, promotes good land use, and encourages stable community development. Farm leaders in the states and local communities have here a special challenge and responsibility.

SOIL CONSERVATION PROBLEMS

Farm leaders are confronted by two sets of issues in the soil-conservation field. They must reach a judgment on the extent of conservation that is economically practicable. Primarily this takes the form of judging how much public money ought to be spent for soil conservation and flood prevention purposes. They also must decide on the relative emphasis to place on extension educational programs, on technical assistance programs of the Soil Conservation Service, on conservation practice-payment programs, and on the use of police power or land-use regulations.

In this matter of appropriate methods it is fruitless to argue that one is superior to all others. Responsible farm leaders will study all available evidence and support the combination of methods that promises to be most economical and effective from time to time.

Farm leaders have a special responsibility with respect to the conservation of resources on public lands. The commonly accepted idea that public ownership assures management policies in the public interest is in error (see Chapter 10). Leadership is needed especially in developing a better basis for determining the true or full public interest with respect to current use and conservation of relatively new arid lands in the Western states.

FARM LEADERSHIP IN GOVERNMENT

Both legislators and administrators exercise leadership with respect to the solution of farm problems. The ethically sensitive legislator has many opportunities to exercise independent initiative and judgment on issues affecting the general welfare while faithfully representing his district. This is inherent in the legislative process. Often the legislator, on the basis of the information available to him, must take a position before the voters in his district are fully informed regarding the issues involved or when he cannot in good conscience comply with the opinion of a majority of them.

Probably about half the farm people in rural areas are members of the general farm organizations. In a democracy such as ours it is highly important to have ethically sensitive representatives who familiarize themselves with the problems and the needs of the unorganized and often disadvantaged individuals in their districts.

Administrators of broadly-worded legislation face equity and economic issues similar to those faced by the legislators in framing the legislation. An administrator in carrying out his program should be fully as sensitive to the ethical issues involved as are, or ought to be, the members of the legislative branch that enacts the legislation. Good administration requires decisions that result in a minimum of inequity and also a minimum of interference with economic forces that promote efficiency and productivity and other desirable goals.

The administrative staff also exercises a key role in proposing additional legislation. Administrators have the same responsibility with respect to unorganized groups and individuals as have the elected representatives in the legislative branch of government.

Effective farm leadership in government as in the farm organizations is based on both a sense of social responsibility and a mastery of the results of scientific analyses of farm problems. Without scientific analyses farm leaders with the best of ethical motivations become blind dogmatists guided primarily by their emotions. On the other hand, no amount of scientific information of itself can assure fair and equitable decisions and the exercise of desirable leadership.

Appendix: Farmer Cooperatives

by Charles H. Seaver

The importance of the many farm organizations engaged in marketing farm products and furnishing farm supplies has been recognized earlier in this volume, as on pp. 78, 94, 103-4 and in many other references. These cooperatives, though most are independent entities, are more or less related historically and currently to the "general" farm organizations that have been given more extensive treatment. But the range, diversity, and complexity of the development of farmer cooperatives precluded adequate treatment of them within the limits of this volume. This appendix may serve to indicate more fully their importance in the agricultural economy, to clarify their relationship to the "general" farm organizations, to indicate the extent and variety of their operations, and to discuss this phase of agriculture from both an economic and an ethical point of view.

American farmers, of course, are concerned with (a) where most economically to purchase the mechanical equipment, fuel, feed, seed, fertilizer, and other necessities for production, and (b) when, where, and how to market their products most advantageously. In many segments of our economy corporate (or cooperative) purchasing or selling has been found preferable to individual action. Labor unions, chain stores, combinations in industry are examples. So, gradually but increasingly, farmers have come to organize cooperative associations for the purposes mentioned, in tune with the "organizational revolution" that has pervaded our economic life.

THE COOPERATIVE PATTERN[1]

The farmers' cooperative associations engaged in marketing, purchasing and/or supplying, or other services are business enterprises organized on a fairly standardized pattern. Most of them are corporations chartered

[1] Some of the subject matter of this section has been adapted from C. Maurice Wieting, *The Progress of Cooperatives* (New York: Harper & Brothers, 1952); from I. Harvey Hull, *Built of Men*, (New York: Harper & Brothers, 1952); and from *The Story of Farmer Cooperatives*, Farmer Cooperative Service (U.S. Department of Agriculture, 1954).

under state laws; they are subject also to general and special federal regulations. They represent a type of competitive private enterprise, though different in some respects from other business corporations.

"A cooperative enterprise," according to one definition, "is one which belongs to the people who use its services, the control of which rests equally with all its members, and the gains of which are distributed to the members in proportion to the use they make of its service." With slight variations this definition is generally applicable. The main differences from other types of business enterprise may be further explained:

1. While the capital needed for the operation of a cooperative is obtained partly from the members who purchase shares, they are entitled only to limited dividends (usually not exceeding 4-6 per cent) out of any excess of income over expenses. Other capital needed is borrowed from banks. Membership is usually open to all who wish to use its services.

2. Control is exercised by the members served. In most cases each member has one vote, regardless of his number of shares or the extent of his use of the service. The members, meeting periodically, elect a board of directors who employ the active management. Proxy voting usually is not allowed.

3. Net income above that required to pay the limited dividends, or as approved working capital or reserves, is distributed to members according to the amount of business done for them. Any underpayments to producers in advances or overcharges are adjusted in the refunds. The cooperative as a corporate entity, while it may have "unallocated surplus" in some years, makes no "profit" accruable to its shareholders in more than the stipulated nominal dividends.

4. Local cooperatives in many cases have combined, or joined larger state or regional cooperatives, which have two main *structural* types. A centrally operated cooperative, with widespread individual membership but fairly stable direction, appears to have certain advantages over looser organizations in the competition with middlemen or manufacturers outside the cooperative fold. It may have substantial resources, its own or affiliated agents and dealers, access to important markets.[2] Another type is the federated structure, whose membership is made up of local coopera-

[2] The Cooperative Grange League Federation Exchange, Inc., of Ithaca, N. Y. (known generally as GLF), with over 100,000 individual members, is a notable example of this type and the largest regional cooperative in America. Operating mainly in New York, New Jersey, and northern Pennsylvania, it has 365 independent agents, 44 independent cooperatives, and 357 retail outlets with which it maintains regular relations, and its sales in 1951 amounted to about $150 million. Its feed mill in Buffalo is the largest in the world. The Southern States Cooperative of Richmond, Va., with 250,000 patrons, is also representative of this type.

tives which the individual farmers control.[3] There are variations of these types, but all have distinctive cooperative elements differentiating them from other business organizations.

According to their *functions*, there are three general classes of farm cooperatives:

1. The *marketing* cooperatives sell the products of their farmer members. They have storage and shipping facilities, and may process some products. They have daily information as to markets available and range of prices, and advise their members also regarding quantity and quality of products marketable. Some of these cooperatives deal only in one kind of product (such as grain, cotton, livestock, fruit, nuts, poultry, milk, etc.);[4] others in several kinds, especially in areas of mixed farming.

2. The *purchasing* or *supply* cooperatives furnish farm supplies—most of them a variety of supplies, ranging from feed, petroleum, seed, fertilizer, insecticides, hardware, farm machinery, even to household supplies. Many of the larger cooperatives, either separately or in conjunction with others, have manufacturing plants and oil refineries. Some cooperatives perform both marketing and supply functions.

3. *Service* cooperatives are organized to enable farmers to meet various other specialized needs—such as credit, insurance, telephones, electricity, irrigation, and medical care.[5]

[3] The Ohio Farm Bureau Cooperative Association, a federated cooperative, which originated in and is closely affiliated with the Farm Bureau but is a legally separate organization, did a business of over $50 million in 1950, partly in marketing grain but more in farm supplies. It owns its own petroleum refineries and fertilizer plants. Another example of the federated type is the Consumers Cooperative Association of Missouri (Kansas City), serving about 1700 local cooperatives and 350,000 members in ten states. Its farm supply business in 1950 amounted to $62 million, about 70 per cent being petroleum products.

[4] There are about 250 of these large-scale commodity cooperatives. A majority of these are organized on a centrally-operated basis. Typical are the Land O'Lakes Creameries (Minn.), the Dairymen's League Cooperative Association (N.Y.), the Pacific Wool Growers (5 states), the National Livestock Producers Association (St. Louis, several states), the Farmers Union Livestock Association (Omaha, several states), the American Cotton Cooperative Association (a federation), and the Florida Citrus Exchange. Cooperatives of this type usually set up their sales offices in principal cities.

[5] In 1954 the 1145 farm loan associations had $1281 million outstanding in mortgage loans, and the 499 production credit associations about $600 million outstanding in short-term production loans. The Farm Credit Administration supervises and backs these associations.

Local farmers' mutual insurance companies existed here more than a century ago. The 1800 farm mutuals, about half of them over 50 years old, have more than $20 billion in force. Many of them invest some of their funds in other cooperatives.

Telephone service, when widely available in other areas, reached rural areas

The trend of both marketing and supplying cooperatives seems to include a shift toward larger associations of centrally operated types which can employ skilled management, obtain better access to markets and sources of supplies, and achieve greater efficiency in the special services they render. Auxiliary associations also have been set up for aid to local or larger cooperatives in such matters as accounting and auditing, market information, educational programs, advertising campaigns, etc.

The "general" farm organizations fully treated in the body of this book have had a large part in establishing, promoting, and protecting the farm cooperative movement in the United States. Important national cooperative organizations also that are specially devoted to this field have emerged during the past thirty years. They have contributed notably to cooperation among cooperatives, to enlistment of government support, to maintenance of the cooperative pattern, and to public understanding of the movement.

The American Institute of Cooperation, organized in 1925, is an educational organization which carries on continuing programs with youth groups, vocational agriculture teachers, and state extension service staffs; sponsors and participates in state, regional, and annual national meetings for consideration of public relations, membership, taxation, and other problems of cooperatives; and aims to develop a widespread public understanding of farmer cooperatives and their place in our private enterprise economy. Its Youth Education Division works closely with the Future Farmers of America and the 4H Clubs.

The National Council of Farmer Cooperatives (1929), succeeding an earlier organization of similar name, holds annual meetings for discussion of important questions of policy and procedures vital to the organization and operation of farmer cooperatives, and works toward

---

slowly. Mutual companies, however, were formed among farmers to provide this service. By 1937 there were about 1800 such companies serving nearly 700,000 rural families.

Electric light and power reached farms even more slowly; the electric utility companies found more profitable opportunities, of course, in other areas. In 1911 less than 11 per cent of farms had this service. Eventually, in 1935, a Rural Electrification Administration was created by Congress to grant government loans to rural electric cooperatives, which in 1953 numbered over 900, serving nearly four million farms. The story of this development has been told by Marquis Childs in *The Farmer Takes a Hand* (New York: Doubleday & Company, Inc., 1952).

The development of cooperative health services has become notable in rural areas, as indeed in urban areas, only within quite recent years. Various patterns of operation are currently used. The "general" farm organizations are promoting such services, and an affiliate of the Cooperative League, as a federation of medical-care cooperatives and consumer-sponsored health plans, is now serving about 600,000 families.

coordination of cooperative agencies with related government agencies (see pp. 103-4). Affiliated with it are 28 state councils.

The Cooperative League, a national federation of cooperative groups of various types, has a largely but not exclusively farmer membership and is devoted mainly to promotion of the cooperative pattern wherever practicable. Much of the cooperative literature and other cooperative educational and promotional material is prepared and sponsored by the League.

THE PRESENT SCOPE OF FARMER COOPERATIVES

The Farmer Cooperative Service of the United States Department of Agriculture has recently compiled and issued a report of its 1952-53 survey of the farmer cooperatives in the United States engaged in marketing, purchasing and supplying, and other services.[6] The survey included about 90 per cent of the bona fide farmer cooperatives. The data in this section are taken from that Report.

There were reported about 6.5 thousand cooperatives engaged principally in marketing farmers' products, with 4.2 million members and participants; 3.4 thousand engaged principally in furnishing farm supplies, with 3.1 million members and participants; 250 providing miscellaneous related services, with 90 thousand members and participants. The total runs to over 10 thousand associations with about 7.5 million members and participants. These are cooperatives marketing farm products, furnishing farm supplies, and providing closely related services.

It is relevant to note in this connection, as was discussed in Chapter 6 of this volume (pp. 45-6), that there were in the United States at the time of the 1949 farm census, out of more than 5 million farms counted, about 2 million "commercial" farms; i.e., "which produced per farm over $2500 worth of products." These farms "accounted for 88 per cent of all farm products marketed." There were about 1 million other farms with lower farm sales but family incomes over $2000. It may be assumed that these two groups include most or nearly all of the membership of the farm cooperatives. Many producers have membership in more than one cooperative.

The Report covered also (from other government sources) other types of farm cooperatives: in the field of production, 3.7 thousand cooperative dairy-cattle breeding and dairy-herd associations, with 634 thousand members and participants (including duplications); and 9.3 thousand mutual irrigation companies, with 148.5 thousand participants. In the field of special farm services not included above were reported (each set

[6] *Statistics of Farm Cooperatives*, U.S. Department of Agriculture (May 1955).

of two numbers showing number of associations and membership respectively): national farm loan associations (1955) 1,111–326,000; production credit associations (1955) 498–476,000; banks for cooperatives (1955) 13–129,000; rural farm credit unions (1954) 200–30,000; farmers mutual fire insurance companies (1953) 1725–3,500,000; rural electric cooperatives (1954) 910–3,908,000; rural health cooperatives (1954) 13–39,000.

More than two thirds of all the farmers in the United States, it has been estimated, belong to cooperatives.[7]

The scope of farm cooperatives is indicated also by the volume of business they do, its variety, and the geographic distribution.

In the fiscal year 1953 the value (at first sale level) of farm products marketed by 7208 cooperatives was about $7.4 billion. The dairy products amounted to nearly $2.5 billion, the leading states in order being Wisconsin, New York, and Minnesota; grain (including soy beans) $1.6 billion, Illinois, North Dakota, and Iowa leading; livestock, $1.5 billion, Illinois, Ohio, and Iowa leading; fruits and vegetables, $596 million, California, Florida, and Washington leading; cotton $380 million, Texas, Mississippi, and California leading; poultry products, $321 million, California, New Jersey, and Minnesota leading. Of the total value of all products marketed by farm cooperatives about 53 per cent was in the twelve North Central states.

In the same year 7418 farm cooperatives furnished farm supplies to their patrons to the amount of $1.9 billion. The main items were feed, $810 million; petroleum products, $422 million; fertilizer, $184 million; seed, $95 million; farm machinery and equipment, $76 million. The leading states in value of sales were, in order, New York, Minnesota, Illinois, Iowa, Ohio, and Pennsylvania.

The net business in related services (such as trucking, packing, storage, etc.) amounted to about $142 million.

Every state in the Union now has both marketing and supplying farm cooperatives. They vary in number from the 5 in Nevada to the 1330 in Minnesota, and in net business done from the $5 million in Nevada to the $843 million in California.

THE HISTORICAL BACKGROUND

Farmers' cooperation in production, marketing their products, and purchasing supplies had a long history in the United States before it became an important organized movement.[8] During the first sixty-odd

---

[7] Wieting, *op. cit.*, p. 14.

[8] It antedated the often-quoted Rochdale consumers' cooperative enterprise, which, however, developed a pattern based on principles that have been reflected in the cooperative movement in the United States and Canada.

years of the nineteenth century there were many local isolated beginnings (besides some organization of the dairy industry in the Northeast and the Mormon enterprise in Utah); but individualism generally prevailed in all aspects of farming, though corporations had begun to make headway in other fields of industry.[9]

After the Civil War the continued westward spread of farming resulted in more production of grain and livestock than the current domestic and foreign markets would take at a tolerable price. The situation was especially acute in the mid-western states; also in the South, with its special postwar problems. Bankers and other money-lenders refused to lend money to the farmers on their crops and charged high rates of interest on farm loans. The tariff-protected manufacturers and their dealers charged excessive prices for farm machinery and supplies. The railroad companies were bitterly accused of exacting unreasonably high rates for carrying farm produce while giving rebates to favored nonfarm shippers. The farmers sought help from their state legislatures, but lacked adequate organization.

The founding of the National Grange, Patrons of Husbandry, in 1867-68, marked the beginning of an extensive farmers' cooperative movement. Starting in New York and Pennsylvania, the Grange spread rapidly westward and southward. By 1874 it claimed over 20,000 locals and 1.5 million members. It was organized as a social and fraternal organization (a pattern eventually resumed); but its leaders soon recognized that under existing farm conditions the organization could not ignore the farmers' need for both political and economic united action. The two chief objectives in action seemed to be the legislative regulation of freight charges and other railroad practices and the promotion of farmers' cooperative marketing associations. While the "Granger" legislation of the 1870s in Midwestern states indicated progress in the political field and gave some assurance of federal regulation of interstate transportation, the spread of farm cooperatives seemed to promise success also in the field of farmers' business organization. But after a few years, with a temporary return of farm prosperity, the Grange's organizing activity nearly ceased and its membership dwindled. And the farm cooperative movement, afflicted with inefficient management, unwise extension of credit, and farmers' desertion, nearly collapsed. There remained, however, a residue of successful cooperatives and of cooperative experience.

[9] The problems and activities of farm groups in this period are briefly described in *The Story of Farmers' Cooperatives, op. cit.*; and in more detail in E. C. Kirtland, *A History of American Life* (New York: F. S. Crofts & Co., 1939), pp. 500 ff; Allen Nevins, *The Emergence of Modern America 1865-1878* (New York: The Macmillan Company, 1927), ch. VI, "The Revolt of the Farmer"; and Morrison and Commager, *Growth of the American Republic* (New York: Oxford University Press, 1940), Vol. II, pp. 207-13.

Though the Grange recovered its momentum early in the 1880s, it shifted its emphasis more to social activities. Other, more aggressive, farm organizations came into the political and economic field. Most notable, for a time, were the Farmers Alliances, which flourished in the 1880s and 1890s but faded out with the Populists or People's party which they had joined. Two new farm organizations founded in 1902 were more durable; the American Society of Equity (now Farmers Equity Union) and the Farmers Educational and Cooperative Union, started in Texas. Both were active in promoting a revival of the farm cooperative movement, especially the Farmers Union (see pp. 101-3). In the 1890s and 1900s many producers of specialized commodities set up cooperative marketing associations; e.g., livestock, orange, grape, wool, cotton, and grain producers. The movement, however, (with a few exceptions) was not yet on a substantial basis.

NEW SUPPORT, NEW GROWTH

The Smith-Lever Act (1914), while not directly aiding cooperatives, provided for grants, to be matched by the states, in aid of agricultural extension. New York had already established a system of county farm bureaus to be organized by the farmers, and several other states had followed. Secretary of Agriculture Houston warned the county bureaus and agents not to participate directly in farm trade organizations, but allowed them to advise and aid them, with certain restrictions. The farmers used the system to encourage the development of organizations for the cooperative purchase of such supplies as fertilizer and the cooperative sale of farm products. The county groups became known as farm bureaus, then were federated into state organizations, and in 1919 into the American Farm Bureau Federation. In 1929, when a Federal Farm Board was set up in the Agriculture Marketing Act, the government was committed also to aid the establishment (including loans) of "a farm marketing system of producer-owned and producer-controlled cooperative associations and other agencies." The local and federated cooperatives established under this impetus enjoyed the sponsorship and guidance of the Farm Bureaus, but had separate legal status. Others that had been or subsequently were established independently, including many large-scale, centrally-operated, and federated cooperatives, and cooperatives related to the Grange or the Farmers Union, had parallel encouragement by the federal government.

The three federal acts important to the farm cooperative movement during the 1920s were the Capper-Volstead Act (1922) officially sanctioning the operation of such farmers' "associations, corporate or otherwise, with or without capital stock, in collectively processing, preparing for market, handling, and marketing . . . such products of persons so engaged . . . provided, however, that such associations are operated for the mutual benefit of the members thereof" and conform to certain stated requirements; the Cooperative Marketing Act (1926), providing for a division of cooperative marketing in the Department of Agriculture, with various functions, including those of the present Farmer Cooperative Service; and the Agriculture Marketing Act (1929) previously mentioned.

The depression in the farm economy that began in the 1920s and continued into the 1930's impeded the operations of some cooperatives, but emphasized the need of cooperative activity. During that period, indeed, some of the strongest regional organizations now functioning were established. The Farm Credit Administration was set up in 1933 to expand the credit system for cooperatives, through Federal Land Banks and the National Farm Loan Credit Association; and at the same time Banks for Cooperatives were established to make operating loans available. A program for helping low-income farmers to form cooperatives was also set up by the Department of Agriculture in the 1930s. Through the latter 1930s and the 1940s, with government encouragement, the membership in marketing, supply, and service cooperatives rose from less than three million to more than seven million.

The story may be ended there. The present situation is indicated in the statistical survey in a previous section. After so many years of ups and downs, the farm cooperatives seem now to have a well established status in the American economy.

Social and Ethical Responsibilities

The social and ethical responsibilities of farm leaders, more particularly the leaders of the "general" organizations, have been discussed in the main body of this volume.[10] Another volume of this series, has been devoted entirely to the social and ethical responsibilities of businessmen, with some incidental references to cooperatively organized business.[11] And the author of still another volume of the series has given a chapter to "the farm organization movement," which received his blessing, though not unalloyed; he included also a colloquy with an ardent cooperative leader.[12] So it would seem that the ground indicated by the title of this section had been well covered.

[10] See pp. 8-10. See also Leadership in Index.
[11] Howard R. Bowen, *The Social Responsibilities of the Businessman* (New York: Harper & Brothers, 1953), pp. 25, 35-6, 43.
[12] Kenneth Boulding, *The Organizational Revolution: A Study in the Ethics of Economic Organization* (New York: Harper & Brothers, 1953), pp. 150-58, 265-67.

For those readers of this book, however, who unfortunately have not read the volumes by Professors Bowen and Boulding, it may be appropriate to include here a few notes about some social and ethical aspects of the farm cooperative movement in particular.

While as a whole the promotion of the cooperative movement as a form of economic organization has been based largely on the prospect of removing economic disadvantages or gaining economic advantages for the participants, it has often had an ethical and religious tinge. Of course, equalization of economic opportunity is in itself an ethical ideal. The ethical emphasis was perhaps most notable in the earlier stages of the movement and in the promotion of consumers' cooperatives. Religious leaders (Protestant, Roman Catholic, and Jewish) have been interested and sympathetic—often actively participating—and there have been numerous official and semi-official endorsements of the cooperative movement by church councils and other church organizations.[13] It has seemed to many advocates and participants to represent an application of the social and religious ideals of democracy and brotherhood to our economic life.

On the basis of social and economic justice, the farm cooperative movement particularly has had repeated endorsement also outside religious organizations. Nearly fifty years ago a commission appointed by President Theodore Roosevelt reported that first among the immediate needs of country life was "effective cooperation among the farmers, to put them on a level with the organized interests with which they do business." And twenty years later President Coolidge, Secretary of Agriculture Jardine, and Secretary of Commerce Hoover were pronouncing farm cooperatives the principal hope of agriculture. At about that time John D. Black, Professor of Agricultural Economics at Harvard, in a notable survey gave as his "final conclusion" that "for agricultural betterment we shall have to wait until we can make our cooperative organizations stronger."[14] The federal legislation of the 1920s, previously mentioned, reflected the increasing recognition of the place of cooperatives in our farm economy.

It was also in the 1920s that the slogan of "commodity marketing" was widely heard in cooperative circles, with the proposal that "large-scale associations be created to handle the entire output of specified crops in the important producing regions. Back of this idea was the unmentioned but implied promise of monopoly control and monopoly prices."[15] This

[13] Benson Y. Landis, *Manual on the Church and Cooperatives* (New York: Federal Council of Churches, 1947); also *The Social Ideals of the Churches for Agriculture and Rural Life*, bulletin of The Christian Rural Fellowship, 156 Fifth Avenue (New York: 1942).

[14] J. D. Black, *Agricultural Reform in the United States* (New York: McGraw-Hill Book Company, 1929), ch. VI.

[15] *The Story of Farmer Cooperatives*, pp. 17-19.

plan spread rapidly, whether or not the "promise of monopoly" was the prevailing and doubtfully ethical motive. Within five years, by 1925, there were 74 such large-scale, centrally controlled associations, with nearly 900,000 members. Many have survived where conditions were especially favorable, but monopolistic control has rarely been achieved or maintained and the interest of the consumer has generally been well served.

The closing of the gap between producers and consumers was cited by Professor Black as an objective of the farm marketing cooperatives. To what extent this has been achieved available statistics do not indicate. The intervening costs of processing, selling, transportation, delivery, etc., have risen rather steadily for consumers, as more services have been provided and as the range of marketing has been widened, without increase of farm incomes. In this situation the interests of farmers, middlemen, and consumers seem difficult to reconcile.

The farm cooperatives have drawn farmers closer together—in their local associations, in special product groups, and in state and national organizations—not merely for occasional or incidental or temporary purposes, but to carry on together the various external relations of the down-to-earth everyday business in which their capital and labor are engaged. The fact of organization itself has important social significance. It develops a sense of community, not only locally but also more widely, and encourages the solution of common problems, as far as possible, by voluntary group action. The cooperative, democratically organized, does not submerge individual responsibility, but tends to equalize individual opportunity in an economy increasingly dominated by corporate organizations.

Whether the democratic philosophy, however, that pervaded the farm cooperative movement from its beginnings has been or can be maintained in the larger and wider-spread cooperative organizations may present a continuing problem. Like other large organizations, they cannot operate efficiently in the traditional manner of New England town meetings. A representative pattern is required, with delegated authority as well as responsibility. And, whatever the supposed safeguards, democratic elements often fade in that pattern—whether in government, corporate business, organized labor, or perhaps even farm cooperatives.

A related problem of equal ethical significance may appropriately be mentioned—though the farm cooperatives cannot do all that is needed for its solution or alleviation. It should offer them, however, not only an added responsibility but also an added opportunity. This is the disadvantaged situation of millions of low-income farmers, most of whom are not included in the cooperative fold—among them tenant farmers in various types of tenancy.[16] While many low-income farmers may well be encouraged to shift to other lines of economic activity, as noted elsewhere in this volume, the wholesale application of this therapy is not desirable or expedient. Insofar as cooperative organization would help assistance in the organization of service, health, marketing, and supply cooperatives in low-income farming areas seems to be an ethical requirement.

The problem of the farm surplus has been fully discussed earlier in this volume.[17] It causes serious concern, of course, to the cooperative as well as the "general" farm organizations, whose memberships are largely identical. The economic, political, social, and ethical issues reach beyond the farms to the nation, and beyond our nation to the turbulent family of nations.

Altogether the farm cooperative organizations, with a membership even greater than that of the general farm organizations, have likewise social and ethical responsibilities which their leaders, though deeply involved in the structure of modern business, cannot safely ignore. And their promotional, educational, and other far-reaching constructive activities show a commendable breadth of social concern.

[16] pp. 73-80, 147-8, 173-4.
[17] pp. 7, 14-6, 24-30. See also Surplus in Index.

Index